V. S. NAIPAUL

by Robert D. Hamner

This is the first volume of the Twayne World Authors Series to be devoted to a West Indian author. For that matter, it is also the first book-length work to be written about novelist V. S. Naipaul. Significant as these "firsts" may be, however, the value of the study does not depend upon them. Since publication of his first novel in 1957, Mr. Naipaul has captured one after another most of the prestigious British literary prizes. Even though his reputation is not yet popularly known in the United States, his various works have steadily won critical acclaim from all parts of the English speaking world.

Combining critical examination with descriptive analysis, this book brings Naipaul's various works into perspective. The satiric thrust of everything he writes—travel books, short stories, and novels—has invited controversy from the beginning. Starting from the Trinidad of his birth and working outward to England, America, and Africa, Naipaul has directed the keen edge of his insight into the heart of numerous individual and social problems. He is best in his eight novels (*The Mystic Masseur, The Suffrage of Elvira, Miguel Street, A House for Mr Biswas, Mr Stone and the Knights Companion, The Mimic Men, A Flag on the Island,* and *In a Free State*) and emphasis is given to these, but no matter what his chosen form of expression he is adept at revealing with pathos, humor, and often with acrid bitterness the inconsistencies and inhumanities of man.

TWAYNE'S WORLD AUTHORS SERIES

A Survey of the World's Literature

Sylvia E. Bowman, Indiana University

GENERAL EDITOR

WEST INDIES

John P. Dyson, Indiana University

EDITOR

V. S. Naipaul

(TWAS 258)

TWAYNE'S WORLD AUTHORS SERIES (TWAS)

The purpose of TWAS is to survey the major writers —novelists, dramatists, historians, poets, philosophers, and critics—of the nations of the world. Among the national literatures covered are those of Australia, Canada, China, Eastern Europe, France, Germany, Greece, India, Italy, Japan, Latin America, the Netherlands, New Zealand, Poland, Russia, Scandinavia, Spain, and the African nations, as well as Hebrew, Yiddish, and Latin Classical literatures. This survey is complemented by Twayne's United States Authors Series and English Authors Series.

The intent of each volume in these series is to present a critical-analytical study of the works of the writer; to include biographical and historical material that may be necessary for understanding, appreciation, and critical appraisal of the writer and to present all material in clear, concise English—but not to vitiate the scholarly content of the work by doing so.

V. S. Naipaul

By ROBERT D. HAMNER

Hardin-Simmons University

Twayne Publishers, Inc.   ::   New York

Preface

At present the most tenable argument identifies West Indian literature as a tradition within a tradition; it is an outgrowth and an extension of the Western tradition of writing. Whether it will ever become something else is as yet a matter of conjecture. But leaving aside the question of indigenous integrity, we ought to give consideration to the artistry of prominent West Indian authors. Emphasis must be placed on individual artists because it is they who influence and shape tradition, whether or not it is "pure."

One of the most gifted and prolific writers of the Caribbean area is Trinidadian Vidiahar Surajprasad Naipaul. Already recognized as a promising young regional author, Naipaul may be on his way to becoming established as one of the finest international writers to have emerged since World War II. His critical reception varies greatly, from exuberant praise to bitter denunciation, as befits the effective satirist who by the very nature of his work must be divisive. The most contentious reviewers, however, usually find something to commend in his writing even when their overall appraisal is negative, and qualified rejection is sometimes refreshing when weighed against book-jacket blurbs.

It should be recognized that in its dealing with Naipaul, criticism itself is also undergoing a kind of trial. Criticism of Naipaul and of all West Indian literature is in its formative stages. Western tradition must continue expanding to enclose yet another healthy offspring. From this enlargement mutual advantage obtains: new blood will flow into the established language, and young talent will get an opportunity to profit from a broader base of experience. The work of increasingly proficient writers such as Naipaul provides a convenient bridge whereby separate cultures may benefit from an enriching exchange of feelings and ideas. It remains now for criticism and

tradition, first, to comprehend him and then to make his contribution more readily available to the reading public.

As one step toward accomplishing this end, the chapters of
this study are devoted to an intensive analysis of the structure
and content of Naipaul's works. Attention will be given to all
his published books, but the primary concern is with his longer
fiction. The short stories, his travel books, and his one historical
work are indispensable adjuncts to the novels, but since it is
as a novelist that Naipaul has established his international
reputation his subsidiary writing, as well received as it has
been in its own right, will be treated separately and will come
into the main body of this study only as it illuminates some
aspect of his fiction.

The opening chapter serves a twofold purpose. This being
the first volume in the Twayne World Authors Series to be
devoted to a West Indian author, it is necessary that a brief
introduction to the geographical area be given. But, primarily,
attention will be focused on short stories collected in *A Flag
on the Island* and *In a Free State*, on the two travel books, *The
Middle Passage* and *An Area of Darkness*, and on the historical
work, *The Loss of El Dorado*. The shorter fiction and to an
even greater extent the three discursive books define and intensify the world out of which Naipaul derives his imaginative
re-creation.

Following this, in Chapter 2, I shall systematically analyze
the structural framework and techniques of each of the eight
novels in the order of their publication; hence the first novel
written, *Miguel Street*, will appear third in order of investigation. Included along with brief plot summaries are analyses of
narrative devices and patterns of emotional development.

Setting and characterization are handled together in the third
chapter; the uniquely colorful West Indian figure is so much
an integral part of his island background that it would be im-
practical to separate them. The verisimilitude of Naipaul's style
necessitates attending to matters of local color, regional dialect,
and the indigenous aspects of certain images, symbols, and motifs.

Chapter 4 concentrates on the satirical humor that sets the
dominant tone of the voice for all the works from the early

farcical ones to the deeper, more somber psychological studies of the later fiction. Individuals and institutions are ridiculed, but beneath even the most glib exteriors of his richest comic treatments there is always a discernible concern for the welfare of human beings.

Themes in the novels range from the dramatization of individual struggles for personal and social identity to less particular but nonetheless recognizable difficulties that arise out of the irreconcilable disparities between harsh reality and man's highest ideals. Chapter 5 delves into the variations on central themes which unify individual books and recur throughout the body of Naipaul's writing. Each new expression of certain basic ideas gives an effect like that produced by incremental repetition; this adds to the meaning and in the process insures continuity for all his work.

Concluding the study is a look at some of Naipaul's discursive commentary on writing and other writers. As evidence contained in each of these chapters tends to confirm, he transcends regional barriers and is a supranational author' with concepts and principles which place him well within the mainstream of contemporary Western thought and literary expression.

ROBERT D. HAMNER

Austin, Texas

ABOUT THE AUTHOR

Robert Daniel Hamner holds the M.A. and Ph.D. degrees from The University of Texas at Austin. He is assistant professor of English and member of the Graduate Faculty of Hardin-Simmons University. While a graduate student, he began to take an interest in Caribbean writing as a portion of British Commonwealth literature. Out of this interest grew a dissertation concentrated on the novels of V. S. Naipaul and publication of other articles.

V. S. NAIPAUL

Acknowledgments

I am indebted to Professor Joseph J. Jones of the University of Texas at Austin for helpful guidance and suggestions throughout the composition of this work. I am indebted also to the librarians in the main library and the Latin American Collection of the University of Texas at Austin for invaluable assistance in locating and procuring for examination material that was not easily obtainable.

For permission to quote copyrighted material from V. S. Naipaul's works, I am grateful to the following:

Alfred A. Knopf, Inc., for United States rights to quote from V. S. Naipaul, *The Loss of El Dorado* (New York, 1970), and *In a Free State* (New York, 1971).

Andre Deutsch, Ltd., Mr. Naipaul's British Commonwealth publisher, for rights to quote from *The Mystic Masseur* (London, 1957), *The Suffrage of Elvira* (London, 1958), *Miguel Street* (London, 1959), *A House for Mr Biswas* (London, 1961), *The Middle Passage* (London, 1962), *Mr Stone and the Knights Companion* (London, 1963), *An Area of Darkness* (London, 1964), *The Mimic Men* (London, 1967), *A Flag on the Island* (London, 1967), *The Loss of El Dorado* (London, 1969), and *In a Free State* (London, 1971).

Curtis Brown, Ltd., for United States rights to quote from V. S. Naipaul, *The Suffrage of Elvira* (London, 1958), *A House for Mr Biswas* (London, 1961), *The Middle Passage* (London, 1962), and *Mr Stone and the Knights Companion* (London, 1963).

Vanguard Press, Inc., for permission to quote from V. S. Naipaul, *The Mystic Masseur* (New York, 1959), and *Miguel Street* (New York, 1959).

Excerpts are reprinted also with permission of the Macmillan Company from *An Area of Darkness* by V. S. Naipaul, Copyright © V. S. Naipaul 1964, 1965; from *The Mimic Men* by V.

V. S. NAIPAUL

S. Naipaul, Copyright © V. S. Naipaul 1967; from *A Flag on the Island* by V. S. Naipaul, Copyright © V. S. Naipaul 1967.

I am grateful to my wife Carol for assistance in typing and proofreading manuscripts.

Contents

Chronology

1932 Vidiahar Surajprasad Naipaul born in Trinidad, August 17.

1950 Left West Indies for study at University College, Oxford.

1955 Married Patricia Ann Hale.

1957 Publication of *The Mystic Masseur.*

1958 Publication of *The Suffrage of Elvira.* Received the John Llewellyn Rhys Memorial Prize for *The Mystic Masseur.* Served as fiction reviewer on the staff of *The New Statesman* until 1961.

1959 Publication of *Miguel Street.*

1960 Returned for the first time to visit Trinidad on a three-month scholarship granted by the government of Trinidad and Tobago. (At the suggestion of Premier Eric Williams, the time was extended, and Naipaul agreed to write a non-fiction book about the West Indies, September 2, 1960–April 7, 1961.)

1961 Publication of *A House for Mr Biswas.* Composition of *The Middle Passage,* the record of his tour of the West Indies. Received the Somerset Maugham Award for *Miguel Street.*

1962 Publication of *The Middle Passage.* Naipaul begins a year-long tour of India in February.

1963 Publication of *Mr Stone and the Knights Companion.*

1964 Publication of *An Area of Darkness,* the report of his Indian excursion. Received the Hawthornden Prize for *Mr Stone and the Knights Companion.*

1967 Publication of *The Mimic Men.* Publication of *A Flag on the Island.*

1968 Received the W. H. Smith Prize for *The Mimic Men.*

1969 Publication of *The Loss of El Dorado.*

1970 *The Loss of El Dorado* selected by *Time* magazine as one of the ten best nonfiction books of the year.

1971 Publication of *In a Free State.*

CHAPTER 1

West Indian Milieu

I West Indian Literature

THERE is considerable debate as to whether there is a West Indian literature per se. The very fact that the argument occurs is a significant advancement, however, when ,we realize that as recently as thirty years ago hardly anyone was aware of the possibility of its existence. The question is largely one of definition, and it divides into two areas of discussion. For one thing, as the Jamaica-born educator, folklorist, poet Philip Sherlock succinctly expresses it, we are not actually dealing with a country.

There is no country called the West Indies but there are 3½ million West Indians. The name, like the Antilles, once referred to the Caribbean archipelago; now it is limited to Jamaica, Trinidad and Tobago, Barbados, the Leeward and Windward Islands, whose 3½ million people share with the rest of the Caribbean the experience of colonialism, slavery and the plantation, but whose particular metropolitan association was with Britain. For this reason West Indians are English speaking, and their social and political institutions are patterned after those of England.[1]

The second difficulty grows directly out of the "Britishness" of the writing coming from the area. There is some question as to whether it is really West Indian or simply British literature transplanted.

The issue as it is currently phrased is relatively new, but writing about the Caribbean dates back to the period in which Columbus reported his discovery of what he took to be a back entrance to India. Early vestiges of the West Indies appear in such established sixteenth- and seventeenth-century authors as Sir Walter Raleigh, William Shakespeare, Christopher Marlowe, Edmund Spenser, and Andrew Marvell. Daniel Defoe's *Robinson*

15

Crusoe (1719), Michael Scott's *Tom Cringle's Log* (1829-33), Anthony Trollope's *West Indies and the Spanish Main* (1859), and J. A. Froude's *The English and the West Indies* (1888) are but a few of the works of the eighteenth and nineteenth centuries which are set in the islands of the Caribbean.

Indigenous writers have also expressed their points of view. Sufficient native poetry existed in 1931 for N. E. Cameron to compile and publish an anthology of poetry covering the period from 1831 to 1931, and in 1949, J. E. Clare MacFarlane released an anthology of Jamaican poetry. In prose fiction several pens became productive at the turn of this century: F. C. Tomlinson, Thomas MacDermot ("Tom Redcam"), and H. G. deLisser were all published by 1914. Prominent among Caribbean writers from the first half of the century are poets Claude McKay and "Tom Redcam," novelist Alfred Mendes (*Pitch Lake*, 1934, and *Black Fawns*, 1935), novelist-historian C. L. R. James (*Minty Alley*, 1936), and leading into the 1950's novelists Vic Reid (*New Day*, 1949), Edgar Mittelholzer (*A Morning at the Office*, 1950), Samuel Selvon (*A Brighter Sun*, 1952), Roger Mais (*The Hills Were Joyful Together*, 1953), and George Lamming (*In the Castle of My Skin*, 1953).

The list could be extended, but volume and number do not constitute literary worth. This sketchy background would be of little value in itself were it not for a relatively recent burgeoning of highly competent writing by a number of British West Indian authors. Thus far the novel has been their most promising literary form, and accordingly a large portion of criticism (including a well-documented volume by Kenneth Ramchand, published in 1970) has been concerned with novelists of the region.[2] And if we date the birth of the West Indian novel in the early 1950's, then we have reason to designate the late 1950's and the 1960's as a renaissance.[3] The abundance of excellent material from this decade led Louis James to declare in 1968, "Seen as a whole, West Indian literature is perhaps the richest and most varied field of writing in English to have emerged since the second world war."[4] This conclusion may be premature; the sudden fruition of this new "literature" is remarkable, but time must temper our perspective as various young writers vie for places in a continually developing tradition.

Identifiable seeds of West Indian tradition were sown at least as early as World War II, and a healthy growth has begun.

We have seen in our lifetime an activity called writing, in the form of the novel, come to fruition without any previous native tradition to draw upon. Mittelholzer and Reid and Selvon and Roger Mais are to the new colonial reader in the West Indies precisely what Fielding and Smollett and the early English novelists would be to the readers of their own generation. . . . They are the first builders of what will become a tradition in West Indian imaginative writing: a tradition which will be taken for granted or for the purpose of critical analysis by West Indians of a later generation.[5]

The progress George Lamming predicts here is assured by works such as he, V. S. Naipaul, Wilson Harris, John Hearne, and several others have produced. The quality of their output has drawn international critical attention; and perhaps more than anything else it is this attention that is needed, if the relatively flourishing condition of West Indian literature is to continue. More careful study by scholars and critics should facilitate its development. To date, however, with few exceptions most of the scholarship devoted to West Indian imaginative writing has taken the abbreviated form of magazine articles, talks, and isolated seminars. This will change; the literature of the area deserves more intensive, sustained investigation.

II *Trinidadian*

Though only ten years old in sovereignty, the two-island nation of Trinidad and Tobago is one of the most progressive of the former British possessions. Centuries of varied colonial history are reflected in its racial and cultural diversity. The population (estimated at 1,040,000 in 1969) is greatly mixed: Negro 44 percent, Indians of East Indian descent 36 percent, with Lebanese, Syrian, Chinese, white and various combinations of these constituting the remaining 20 percent.[6] Religions include Catholic, Protestant, Hindu, and Islam in close proximity, and sometimes even in conjunction with each other. Trinidad claims to have given the world the Calypso, steel bands, and the Limbo, but its greatest contribution to culture may yet prove to be in literature.

This growing country has already a number of internationally recognized authors to its credit: Michael Anthony, for example, or C. L. R. James or Samuel Selvon. One of the most prolific and gifted of these Trinidadians is V. S. Naipaul. Naipaul is a third-generation West Indian descended from East Indian immigrant grandparents who sought work in Trinidad's cane fields. His residence on the island terminated in 1950, when at the age of eighteen he took a scholarship to study at Oxford University. After receiving his B.A. degree he remained in London except for brief excursions abroad, steadily publishing eight novels, two travel books, a history, one collection of short stories, and assorted reviews and articles. Currently he lives in the country, not far from Salisbury and Stonehenge.

Naipaul's first published novel, *The Mystic Masseur* (1957), won for him the John Llewellyn Rhys Memorial Prize. He followed with *The Suffrage of Elvira* (1958) and *Miguel Street* (1959). This third book, a series of interconnected sketches in the manner of Anderson's *Winesburg, Ohio,* was written prior to the first two published works but did not see print until Naipaul's reputation was established. It received the Somerset Maugham Award for 1961. His longest and perhaps most accomplished novel to date is *A House for Mr Biswas* (1961). The same pungent satire and subtle humor marking earlier works are more fully developed in the story of Mohun Biswas, a defeated and suffering human being who endures and in the face of absurdity converts the inexplicable tragedy of his life into a truly classic comedy.

The setting of Naipaul's fifth work of fiction is a complete break from the West Indian background of his earlier novels. *Mr Stone and the Knights Companion* (1963)—sandwiched between a travel book of the West Indies, *The Middle Passage* (1962) and the record of Naipaul's visit to the India of his forefathers, *An Area of Darkness* (1964)—is set in contemporary London. In conjunction with the change of scene, there is a corresponding alteration in the protagonist; Mr. Stone, a typical Naipaul creation in other respects, is divested of all West Indian characteristics. He is an elderly British librarian who is confronting the trauma of retirement. These drastic alterations are managed with such artistic precision and ease that the book cap-

tured the oldest of the famous British literary prizes, the Hawthornden Prize, for 1964.

Experience in depicting the British perspective was valuable
in writing *The Mimic Men* (1967). This account of a West
Indian political exile in London uses emotions "recollected in
tranquillity" to trace the boyhood, education, career, and forced
retirement of Ralph Singh (an anglicization for Ranjit Kripal-
singh). This mimic man with a unique identity crisis travels
intermittently from his native island of Isabella to urban London
and back again. His rootlessness in both geographical localities
dramatically represents an integral aspect of man's plight, his
losing touch with reality in the complexities of social living.
This incisive probing of two of the societies closest to Naipaul
brought him the W. H. Smith Prize for literature in 1968.

Naipaul's next publication, *A Flag on the Island* (1967), was
a collection of short stories of uneven quality, some of which had
appeared earlier in periodicals as far back as 1950. It was not
until 1971 that he produced another fictional work, *In a Free
State*, a book which contains, in addition to the title novella, two
short stories and two sections from Naipaul's travel journals. It
continues the diversification of scene and character-nationality
that has figured increasingly in his later writing. But in the
interval between *A Flag on the Island* and *In a Free State*, he
makes his first attempt at writing history. *The Loss of El Dorado*
(1969)—selected by *Time* magazine as one of the ten best
nonfiction books of 1970—is an imaginative study of the Spanish,
French, and British presence in and around Trinidad from
Columbus' discovery to the early nineteenth century.

As in his previous nonfiction, the hand of the novelist is
prevalent in *The Loss of El Dorado*. Naipaul again selects and
organizes his material so that the reader shares not only in the
acquisition of inert facts but in the moods and feelings elicited
in the author as he views his subject. What is lost of scientific
objectivity is more than compensated by his richly suggestive
interpretation.

From the first, his interpretative skill has rendered his discursive works especially valuable to literary scholars. Both
Naipaul's world and a portion of his *Weltanschauung* are skillfully interwoven with each other. His candid indictments of

Caribbean society in *The Middle Passage* and of India in *An Area of Darkness* are well taken; he delves into his subjects intimately and discloses their weaknesses. Authorities familiar with these areas corroborate his assessments for the most part, even when they sometimes disapprove of his reactions to extant problems.

The Middle Passage is not the first travel book to have been written about the West Indies; it comes in the wake of others— James Anthony Froude, Anthony Trollope, Charles Kingsley, Alec Waugh, James Pope-Hennessy, and Patrick Leigh Fermor are among the foreigners who have visited and recorded the area. No small part of the value of Naipaul's book is the fact that it comes from a native of the region, and the view from within is not particularly gratifying. The title itself derives from the middle leg of the ancient trade route which delivered slaves to the New World. Slavery was bad enough, but that which has superseded it—the voluntary servitude of twentieth-century colonialism—still leaves much to be desired. Because of the candor with which Naipaul develops this theme, fellow West Indian Edward Lucie-Smith confesses that he finds the book uncomfortable. "The real reason why I found the book uncomfortable (though very often admirable) is that Mr. Naipaul tackles from the inside the problem which most writers of West Indian travel books have been glad to ignore or glide over—the intricate, strangling relationship between three things: class, race, and colonialism."[7]

At each major stop on his journey—at Trinidad, British Guiana, Surinam, Martinique, and finally Jamaica—Naipaul seems to have been deeply affected by the philistinism of the West Indian middle classes. Time-honored subservience to distant mother countries has ingrained a basic self-contempt that stifles community pride. In the long middle section on British Guiana, he states with good reason that the missionary's first step is to teach self-contempt. "It is the basis of the faith of the heathen convert" (156).[8] Christianity is merely a part of the colonial conditioning which elevates the faith and the race of the white ruling class to the detriment of the remainder of the populace. The effects are still felt in the country's politics. Naipaul seems to have been favorably impressed with the progressive efforts of Cheddi and Janet Jagen to implement government programs under the strictures of a depressed agrarian economy. To add to their problems, the people have not yet adjusted to democracy; even though they exercise the right to vote, they expect government to remain as paternalistic as it was in the past. "Every new voter regards himself as a pressure group. In this way the people—not the politician's abstraction, but the people who wish to beg, bribe and bully because this is the way they got things in the past—in this way the people are a threat to responsible government and . . . to their own leaders. It is part of the colonial legacy" (120).

Moving on to Surinam, Naipaul touches upon other remnants of this legacy. The natural identity of a subject people becomes distorted under colonialism. "True, there is talk about West Indian culture, but this is ingenuous where it is not political, and is rooted in the colonial attitude which rejects as barbarous all that does not issue from the white mother country" (169). His general observation is borne out in the persons of Corly and Theresia, two native residents who carefully maintain their ignorance of, and diffidence toward, local custom and folk tradition. In Martinique the situation is no better. Passing from the former Dutch colony to French territory, Naipaul feels that he has suddenly been transported to France. Even the milk for daily consumption is flown in by Air France, and locally produced rum is not exported directly to its markets but is distributed through agents in Paris. It is, in fact, their assumed "Frenchness" that ultimately unifies the inhabitants of the island.

Further erosion of identity, for Martinique and other parts of the Caribbean as well, comes through tourism. Once the islands were exploited for their wealth; now the descendants of slaves are being dispossessed because of the beauty of their adopted islands. "Every poor country accepts tourism as an unavoidable degradation. None has gone as far as some of these West Indian islands, which, in the name of tourism, are selling themselves into a new slavery" (191). Tourists at once intensify the disparities between rich and poor and force their own tastes and values on those who wish to gain by satisfying these foreign demands. Naipaul's brief stint as guest in an elegant Jamaican

resort brings home both of these liabilities. His airtight,
glassed-in rooms—isolated from the surrounding slums, unem-
ployment, squalor, racial unrest, and of course the tropical
climate—contain all the modern conveniences the affluent visitor
could desire.

Naipaul's final note of disappointment and disgust indicates
that his seven months' tour has done nothing to remove the
uneasiness to which he confesses early in *The Middle Passage*.
His most explicit and severest statements on the West Indian
situation are directed toward the land he knows most intimately:

Trinidad was and remains a materialist immigrant society, continually
growing and changing, never settling into any pattern, always re-
taining the atmosphere of the camp . . . not an expanding society
but a colonial society, ruled autocratically if benevolently, with the
further limitations of its small size and remoteness. All this has
combined to give it its special character, its ebullience and irresponsibility. And more: a tolerance which is more than tolerance: an
indifference to virtue as well as to vice. (54)

This indifference to virtue and vice often expresses itself in a
cynical contempt for distinctions of race and class. What would
have been the colony's upper class has always been absent.
Without its guidance, no local standards could stabilize; each
individual was left to his own devices. The result is the island's
colorful but chaotic amalgamation of races, classes, religions,
and "characters." The passkey to success and local esteem is
money; and how it is obtained does not matter. Outside of
sports and music, little other recognition is prized. Education is
sought for its pragmatic value; knowledge is good only insofar
as it is useful. With other avenues of advancement being closed
to the poor and uneducated (by and large a majority), the
individual's surest methods of getting attention are through cunning and personal eccentricities. "In the immigrant colonial
society, with no standards of its own, subjected for years to
the second-rate in newspapers, radio and cinema, minds are
rigidly closed; and Trinidadians of all races and classes are
remaking themselves in the image of the Hollywood B-man.
This is the full meaning of modernity in Trinidad" (61).

In registering his opinion of this amorphous society, Naipaul is frequently given to broad generalizations—as his critics have not failed to point out. Yet for all his sweeping statements, he seldom fails to introduce specific evidence for support. This may come in the form of quotations from the local press or radio, as pertinent anecdotes drawn from people he meets, or—utilizing his novelist's eye for revealing detail—in his vividly sketched individuals. Naipaul seems to be well aware of his serious role as a writer, not only as recorder but also as synthesizing agent. "Living in a borrowed culture, the West Indian, more than most, needs writers to tell him who he is and where he stands. Here the West Indian writers have failed" (68). In this light, Naipaul's "generalizations" in *The Middle Passage* might just as well be described as summaries. He is formulating problems so that they may be afterward handled more effectively. For example, as he sees it, the major difficulty facing the writer who wishes to portray the West Indian middle class is this group's delusion of whiteness. "They would have to be treated as real people with real problems and responsibilities and affections . . . but they would also have to be treated as people whose lives have been corrupted by a fantasy which is their cross. . . . The gifts required, of subtlety and brutality, can grow only out of a mature literature; and there can be advance towards this only when writers cease to think about letting down their sides" (69).

Naipaul's independence from "sides" is evident. In fact, for criticizing his homeland he has drawn bitter retorts from staunch nationalists who demand complete loyalty to, and support for, their causes. Ronald Bryden, on the other hand, argues that "the brightest prospect for the West Indies and countries like them is the pitying, uncompromising rejection of Mr. Naipaul."[9] As sensitive to human nature as Naipaul's prose shows him to be, he must have anticipated the extremely mixed reactions that were sure to follow publication of *The Middle Passage*. There is not much of pity in the book, but there is obvious concern. It is commendable, in spite of his own deep feelings, the degree to which he manages to concentrate his "gifts of subtlety and brutality," not to place blame or to settle old grievances, but rather to diagnose the problems besetting colonial and former colonial societies.

III *Indian*

On leaving Coronie, in Surinam, Naipaul coins a phrase to describe a decrepit old East Indian whom he had found there waiting to die—"A derelict man in a derelict land" (190). The man has left India so far back in his memory that it now seems magical and hardly tangible. He has made the middle passage, and he has never again found a soil into which he could sink roots. Naipaul apparently has experienced something of the same kind of haunting rootlessness. He says as much in *An Area of Darkness*, his second travel book, the record of his agonizing search through India for the source of his heritage. "India had in a special way been the background of my childhood. . . . It remained a special, isolated area of ground which had produced my grandfather and others I knew who had been born in India and had come to Trinidad as indentured labourers, though that past too had fallen into the void into which India had fallen" (29).

In order to discover more of himself, Naipaul has chosen to return to the land of his ancestors, but no sooner does he step ashore than he feels his identity disintegrate. "It was like being denied part of my reality. Again and again I was caught. I was faceless. I might sink without a trace into that Indian crowd. I had been made by Trinidad and England; recognition of my difference was necessary to me. I felt the need to impose myself, and didn't know how" (46). From the beginning, *An Area of Darkness*, then, is a book as much about the author as it is about India. The "real" India, of course, is not pushed to the background; it is too vast and imposing for that. As a matter of fact, some reviewers have been so impressed with the overall accuracy of Naipaul's observations that they consider this to be one of the best books to have been written about the country. One argues: "This truly dark book contains more of India than has ever been encompassed in so few pages," and critics, "would do well to pause before heaping abuse on him [Naipaul] for his obtuseness and pessimism; for he has revealed, more successfully than any other recent writer, some of the most important socio-psychological facets of the problems with which the progressives are trying to cope."[10]

Not all reviewers are this generous. Insofar as Naipaul's work is accurate, it is an accurate presentation of the effect of India on an articulate, westernized sensibility. Naipaul is definitely unsympathetic toward eastern life styles (especially one perverted by colonialism), and for this reason, those critics who dwell upon his oversights are quite correct.[11] It just happens that no one sees all that is India. In capturing as much as he does, Naipaul very wisely attempts only to assimilate and organize representative portions of the chaos that confronts him. He is prone to make generalizations as in *The Middle Passage,* but again he is at his best when exercising his skills as a novelist, illustrating his points and supporting conclusions by dramatically portraying the issues that seem most important.

From what he sees, Naipaul surmises that Indians are unable or unwilling to look at things directly. To the countless defecating Indians on beaches, river banks, streets, and by railways, everyone is oblivious. After the long trek to the Cave of Amarnath, to view the ice *lingam,* symbol of Shiva, it does not matter to the faithful pilgrims that the ice phallus has melted, is not there; they see it anyway. "A physical growth, because it was extraordinary, was a spiritual symbol. The growth failed; it became the symbol of a symbol. In this spiralling, deliquescing logic I felt I might drown" (180). Naipaul does not settle for pointing out these instances of the Indian's ability to see only what he chooses to see; he records innumerable encounters and describes the reactions of those around. Moreover, as his evidence continues to mount, he manages to convey the sense of his own increasing exasperation.

Some of the most lively portions of the book center around India's debilitating imitation of other countries. "It is the special mimicry of an old country which has been without a native aristocracy for a thousand years and has learned to make room for outsiders, but only at the top" (60). Naipaul sees this mimicry borne out in the outdated dress and slang of English-speaking Indians, in their patronizing attitude toward their own art, in the anglicized names and the imported magazines and newspapers that adorn the up-to-date sitting room. C. D. Narasimhaiah seizes upon this point and upon Naipaul's objections to certain Indian customs to complain of an apparent

inconsistency. "He blames us as much for being only Indians as
for not being wholly Indian."[12] There is no real contradiction;
Naipaul is selective in his condemnations. He dislikes customs
which retard growth and cause public nuisances (not to mention
health hazards), and he disapproves the adoption of meaningless
forms and affectations. In the delightful long second part of
An Area of Darkness, we are shown Mr. Butt's Liward Hotel.
It is billed as modern, with a "flush system." By making the
advertisement, he satisfies the formality, but it is not until
Naipaul arrives and forces the issue that the system is uncrated
and installed.

Another of Naipaul's general conclusions seems to follow
naturally from the two just noted. Unable to look at their country
directly, Indians tend to retreat into fantasy and develop a
fatalistic view of life. Instead of attempting to cope with extant
problems, they comfort themselves with legends of an idyllic
past, and go on imitating the examples set by foreigners. Naipaul
contends that the sad element of Indian history is the absence
of growth and positive development. "India's strength, her ability
to endure, came from the negative principle, her unexamined
sense of continuity. It is a principle which, once diluted, loses
its virtue. In the concept of Indianness the sense of continuity
was bound to be lost. The creative urge failed. Instead of
continuity we have the static" (229).

Harsh as these pronouncements may be toward India, it would
be unfair to the scope and intention of *An Area of Darkness* to
disregard the fact that much of what Naipaul has to say is also
directed toward himself. As Henry Reed expresses it, "Mr.
Naipaul records, candidly and ruthlessly, what he hated there,
and what it made him hate in himself—his reactions of near-
hysteria, disgust and panic; and above all, perhaps, his guilt
at an incapacity for charity, a guilt which his recognition of a
genuine Indian sweetness of disposition and behavior could only
redouble."[13] In one of his more introspective passages, Naipaul
reflects that the type of negativism and passivity which afflicts
the Indian mind has come to possess his life, has given him, too,
a "philosophy of despair."

It is only now, as the impatience of the observer is dissipated in the
processes of writing and self-inquiry, that I see how much this

philosophy had also been mine. It had enabled me, through the stresses of a long residence in England, to withdraw completely from nationality and loyalties except to persons; it had made me content to be myself alone, my work, my name (the last two so different from the first); it had convinced me that every man was an island. (198)

Farther on, after his journey through India, he confesses that the trip should not have been made, that "it had broken my life in two" (280). Seeking roots in the land of his forebears, even to the village from which his grandfather had come, has proved a complete failure. Neither in the physical terrain nor in the realm of the mind has he been able to confirm his identity. But even in recognizing his detachment, he gains a dimension of awareness. "It was only now, as my experience of India defined itself more properly against my own homelessness, that I saw how close in the past year I had been to the total Indian negation, how much it had become the basis of thought and feeling. . . . I felt it as something true which I could never adequately express and never seize again" (281).

IV   *Fools' Gold*

It is not until 1969 that Naipaul publishes his next work of nonfiction. But with the completion of *The Loss of El Dorado* he reveals still another of the many facets of his versatile mind; he ventures into the discipline of the historian. In several respects, this book is better than *The Middle Passage* and *An Area of Darkness*. It retains the same carefully etched flavor of reality and vigorous life of the previous travel books, yet it seems less influenced by the author's personality. Naipaul speaks throughout the work; his passing remarks provide invaluable aids in the sorting out of masses of information, but he has learned to allow the ironies of the story he is recounting to convey their own impact.

The theme dominating this complex history is relatively simple and may be described as "man's futile attempts to grasp the illusions of his own fantasy." In order to give manageable size and shape to events during the four centuries following Columbus' voyages to the new world, Naipaul chose to develop the

implications surrounding two obscure stories. The first concerns
the last phases of the search for the fabled El Dorado, in and
around Trinidad from 1595 to 1617. The second occurs nearly
two hundred years later, at a time when imperialist Britain is
using Trinidad as a base to foment revolution on the South
American continent.

So little information about the background of this area is
readily available to the general public that Naipaul cannot rely
upon a common store of knowledge. In order to re-create the
life of the times, he must not only introduce new names but
he must also show why and how they are vital to an understanding of the development of the region. The search for
El Dorado, as Naipaul points out, is largely the story of Sir
Walter Raleigh. It is also the story of the Spanish conquistador
Antonio de Berrio, and of his lieutenant Domingo de Vera who
originally takes possession of Trinidad in the name of his king
and his general. These are but the first of many who spend their
fortunes and their lives in trying to find the mythical golden
city. Their quests consist of a series of inadequate preparations,
false starts, and pyrrhic victories. One Spanish governor after
another attempts to settle and guard his base on Trinidad and
beat competitors to his goal. Raleigh comes and goes, other
foreigners immigrate, some to make homes, and, finally, after
three hundred years of tenuous Spanish control, Trinidad is
handed over to the British without a struggle.

The change occurs as just part of the political turmoil of the
last quarter of the eighteenth century—the American revolution
begun in 1776, the French in 1789 and the Haitian in 1791.
England, Spain, and France are again engaged in war, and future
control of the West Indies is in grave doubt. Ironically, governor
José Maria Chacon believes that he is merely buying time and
saving lives by surrendering Trinidad to the British forces under
General Abercromby and Colonel Picton. "In 1797 England
looked defeated. Chacon thought that the war was almost over
and that the peace treaty would restore the island to Spain. He
thought he had saved it from France and the republican French,
so dangerous to the Spanish Empire" (122). He is wrong; the
British retain their dominance from that date.

Picton, who succeeds to governorship of the island, proceeds with British plans to establish a lucrative agricultural colony, based on imported slave labor. The new vision of El Dorado, then, is attended by the nightmare of slavery; and slavery is to spread. Preparations are under way for a series of popular revolutions that will draw one South American country after another into the expanding British Empire. Trinidad figures in this larger scheme as a supply depot and a base of operations. As has always been the case, however, ambitious projections for this colony tend to degenerate rapidly. Thus, Picton's story becomes one of petty intrigue, senseless torture, and abortive invasions. It includes the names of such prominent figures as Toussaint L'Ouverture and Francisco Miranda, Napoleon and Wellington (Picton dies a hero years later at Waterloo); yet of more immediate importance in his story is an insignificant mulatto teen-ager, Luisa Calderon.

Luisa Calderon is of the West Indies, of the people, not white, but, by her mixed birth, one remove from slavery. Falsely accused of theft by her vengeful, jealous lover, she is arrested, questioned, and tortured. She survives and even lives to recount her ordeal before a court in England, but her case, not at all an unusual one, is utilized by Picton's enemies to remove him from his governorship. In the name of humanity, Picton is reprimanded, then cleared of blame; Luisa receives momentary sympathy and attention, then drops out of sight. The details are scattered, and until Naipaul seeks them out, have been forgotten.

But the pattern of events is revealing, indicative of the type of relationship that is likely to develop between a colonialist nation and a subject people. As Picton's trial drags on in London, interest lags, and by the time he is finally acquitted, the news is anticlimactic. So it goes with Trinidad. With no advantageous revolution in the offing, the attentions of empire builders settle elsewhere. As Naipaul explains it in the prologue: "It was a failure. The South American revolution took on a life of its own; Port of Spain didn't become the great British trading port for an independent South America. And even at the time of the torture of Luisa Calderon the British Empire was shifting east, to Asia. The slave islands in the west were soon to be run down, and Port of Spain was once again a remote municipality. It was the end of the adventure" (4).

Even before entering on the body of the text, Naipaul thus reveals the end of the narrative he is about to begin. The style of his prose is also beginning to establish a pattern. Interconnecting and woven throughout the two central episodes in the history there is a complex tracing of minor threads, events and people of striking similarity, that emerge and drop away only to reappear again. The general effect is like that of an intricate and varied but thematically unified tapestry. In fact, in the words of Neil Millar, "It is history as fine art rather than history as an academic discipline."[14]

In general, the debate among critics and reviewers centers around the hybrid nature of *The Loss of El Dorado*. No one disputes the scholarship and research; no one denies the vividness of the presentation. Yet the book is a novelist's history, and as such it (like the travel books before) elicits mixed reactions: Phoebe Adams praises the adroitly reconstructed historical characters and the readability of the text; Ronald Bryden condemns the unceremonious manner in which minor figures are "yanked on and off the stage with scarcely the courtesy of an introduction"; and J. H. Elliott feels that "the clipped sentences become monotonous; the constant shifts of focus grow bewildering; the lack of structure makes the book at times hard going, and even slightly dull."[15]

From "living" and "graceful," then, to "dull," the opinions are registered. The book may be too complex to be enjoyable for the careless reader, but as J. H. Plumb observes, no matter how far it may be removed from professional history, "it often presents truths about society that are both more profound and more moving."[16] Naipaul the novelist stresses the human element in his history, just as he has in his travel books. It is fortunate that he has done so. Whatever area of the world Naipaul studies, he attends to the personalities of the individuals he finds there. Much of what he learns, he records in his discursive writing, and this is good, but what is more important, in the process, he opens up both the background of his own development and of the world of his fiction.

In *The Middle Passage* is contained Naipaul's version of today's West Indies; in *An Area of Darkness* is a perceptive, though highly personal, description of contemporary India; then, bringing together Europe and South America, in *The Loss of El Dorado* is a critical look at the early, formative years of the emerging Third World. And in the fiction, too, novels and short stories, the same intimate, cosmopolitan awareness reveals itself.

V *Cosmopolitan*

Critics and reviewers have had little to say about the stories collected in *A Flag on the Island*. The title novella, dated by Naipaul as the latest entry in the book (1965), is usually singled out for analysis, and the other pieces receive passing mention, each critic noting one or more that strikes his fancy. Each of the stories, though not especially remarkable, has merit, and a few are quite successful. Spanning Naipaul's early writing career from 1950 to the early 1960's, they offer a limited sampling of his themes, of his techniques of style and characterization, and of his amazing versatility as a writer of fiction.

Settings alternate between English and West Indian; characters are, without exception, middle class—Indians and whites for the most part—but a black man narrates his own tale in "The Baker's Story"; themes vary, of course, but are consistently developed out of the psychological problems of more or less eccentric figures. Several contain humorous elements: "The Baker's Story," "The Night Watchman's Occurrence Book," and "The Raffle" are light in tone, while "Greenie and Yellow," "The Enemy," and "The Heart" are predominantly somber.

"The Night Watchman's Occurrence Book" (1962) is a tour de force, a delightful vignette presented in the form of a semi-literate hotel clerk's written reports to his employer, Mr. Inskip. Comedy enters through the watchman's naïveté, his broken dialect, and the way in which he innocently disrupts both the hotel's disreputable night business and Mr. Inskip's illicit love affair. Though there is a certain degree of local color in the setting of this story, the events might conceivably have occurred almost anywhere. "Greenie and Yellow" (1957) displays peculiarities of place (it is set in a London tenement house), but the human nature it discloses might be found in any part of the Western world. Mrs. Cooksey, the landlady, officiously interferes in the lives of her pet birds. Childless and lonely (even with her husband), she decides to enforce companionship on "Bluey" and "Greenie" and then attempts to create love between "Greenie" and a new female, "Yellow." Under her surveillance three healthy birds sicken and two die, leaving behind a crippled and forlorn "Bluey." The pathos in her futile gestures is tastefully subdued by Naipaul, and the touches of mild humor round out the story very effectively.

In "The Heart" (1960), geographical location is of little consequence. Richard Plant sees this story and "Greenie and Yellow" as "psychological horror stories."[17] The center of interest is Hari, a rich, spoiled child who, because of his delicate heart condition, is sheltered and cut off from the activities of other children. In his artificial isolation, he is denied the normal outlets for expressions of love, hate, fear, and aggression. As a result, he develops a perverted sense of values. When a small dog is given to him, he quickly assumes the characteristics of a vengeful tyrant. "Soon he extended his judgment to all the puppy's actions, punishing those he thought unfriendly, disobedient or ungrateful. . . . But there were also days when punishments were forgotten, for Hari knew that he controlled the puppy's power and made it an extension of his own, not only by his punishments but also by the complementary hold of affection" (130-31). The ambivalence of his emotional attachments is matched by his irrational actions. He is in the habit of constantly beating the puppy as though he hates it, yet when informed of the puppy's accidental death, he breaks into tears. From the way that Naipaul handles the scene, it is apparent that though the tears may stem from a species of love, the source is not altogether healthy or pure.

Some of the stories in *A Flag on the Island* are more limited as to where they might reasonably have happened; "The Mourners" (1950), "My Aunt Gold Teeth" (1954), and "The Enemy" (1955) definitely reflect the Indian influences of Naipaul's Port of Spain childhood; "Greenie and Yellow" and "The Perfect Tenants" to a lesser extent seem appropriate to certain areas of London. But in everything that he writes, Naipaul's primary concern is to disclose the predicament of human beings.

This trend is underscored in *In a Free State,* both in the travel-book sketches of the "Prologue" and "Epilogue," and in the two short stories "One out of Many" and "Tell Me Who to Kill." Whether on a Mediterranean cruise ship, in Egypt, in London, or in Washington, D.C., the characters are all suspended ambivalently in "free states." Santosh, hero of "One out of Many," makes the transition from street-life in Bombay to the artificial Washington environment, yet he has to confess that "Americans have remained to me, as people not quite real, as people temporarily absent from television" (37). Escaping from his insulated government job and attempting to achieve freedom by acting independently, he discovers only that he is abandoned and alone. The narrator of "Tell Me Who to Kill" fares no better. His move is from the Caribbean to London, and his unsettling discovery is that he cannot distinguish his enemies: "O God, show me the enemy. Once you find out who the enemy is, you can kill him. But these people here they confuse me. Who hurt me? Who spoil my life? Tell me who to beat back" (107). Circumstances thwart his concerted schemes until—and Naipaul only vaguely suggests the details—he can never return to his home. There has been a murder in his past, committed by him or his brother Dayo, but he appears to have assumed the guilt. At his suggestion, the message has been sent home that he is dead.

Like these fictional characters, the tramp in the "Prologue" and the tourists in the "Epilogue" are also drifting about on the surface of life, observers incapable of catching hold of the human reality. In the final section, it is satisfying to find Naipaul himself breaking the established pattern. Taking matters into his own hand, he attempts to save a group of hungry urchins from an Egyptian's whip. The act is merely a gesture, an outgrowth of frustration and anxiety, but it rounds off the volume with a personal touch.

Again, as in most of Naipaul's work, fact and fiction are drawn in close proximity. Not surprisingly, the overall fictional picture largely complements the more direct one of the nonfictional books. In effect, Naipaul submits two parallel views, both equally accurate, of the same reality; and penetrating insights are available from each perspective. Caution must be observed, however, despite the temptation to transfer his discursive judgments to the semiautobiographical but imaginative world of fiction. Naipaul himself was concerned about the consequences of confusing actual with created realities in close proximity. His trepidation almost kept him from writing *The Middle Passage*.

The novelist works towards conclusions of which he is often unaware . . . To analyse and decide before writing . . . would be the opposite of my method as a novelist. I also felt it as a danger that, having factually analysed the society as far as I was able, I would be unable afterwards to think of it in terms of fiction and that in anything I might write I would be concerned only to prove a point. (5)

Naipaul decided to take the risk and his subsequent work, fictional and nonfictional alike, bears witness to his remarkably successful dexterity.

CHAPTER 2

Structural Patterns

I Methods of Construction

BETWEEN *The Mystic Masseur* and publication of *In a Free State*, the structural organization of Naipaul's several novels has undergone a series of discernible changes. There is a marked difference between the early and late fiction, but the alterations in technique reveal a consistent development. Employing rather traditional plots and standard narrative exposition, he offers little that is innovative in the way of structure. In each book, whether the action is presented in simple, straightforward narration or through a complex juxtaposition of episodes which assume significance accumulatively, Naipaul very carefully interrelates the various threads of his chosen plot.

Reduced to chronological outline, Naipaul's novels appear disarmingly simple. The basic framework does not rely for its effect on intricate complexity or on any "high seriousness" of action. Naipaul's primary focus is in his characters; all else depends upon them, and in recounting their experiences he is concerned that he tell their story well. Significantly, four of the published novels are presented through the eyes of a participating narrator. This contributes to the immediacy of these books, making the speaker's personality and the pattern of his emotional development an integral factor in the form of the works. At the same time, viewed from another perspective the narrator functions more as a device for continuity than as a fictional person; his point of view, his tone of voice, and his esthetic distance (not to be confused with that of the author) then assume importance as avenues through which the critic can view the work's basic structural arrangement.

Despite the numerous similarities among Naipaul's novels, each work follows its own design and presents its own special problems. *Miguel Street* may not even qualify strictly as a novel because of its apparent formlessness, and the title stories in *A Flag on the Island* and *In a Free State*, considering their brevity, might best be classified as novelle. Yet such obvious differences in no way detract from the basic cohesiveness of Naipaul's fiction as a whole. Individual works show interesting variations, but they adhere to an underlying pattern which becomes more definite with each additional publication.

II   The Mystic Masseur

First to be published, *The Mystic Masseur* sets the tone for the early novels. The story of Ganesh Ramsumair, the masseur, is ironic. His rise to eminence and recognition as a Member of the British Empire follows from a succession of personal failures. Unable to retain his first job as a teacher, he contentedly resigns himself to drifting about aimlessly. His life takes direction only when others lend impetus. Ramlogan, a father anxious to situate his "second and best" daughter in the proper caste, not only guides Ganesh into marriage, but also suggests that he become a masseur.

Unassertive as he is by nature, he is again on the verge of failure when a distant aunt, "The Great Belcher," gives positive direction to his career. It is she who starts Ganesh as a mystic. "Ganesh make to be a lot more than a ordinary pundit. If he is a Hindu he must realise by now that he have to use his learning to help out other people" (110). Taking this hint, he changes tactics, and miraculously his fame soon spreads until he is known throughout the Caribbean.

A man that popular could not remain out of public service. He is swept by the forces of political intrigue into elective office, to international recognition, and ultimately to final disillusionment. He discovers that political power is insignificant, that he cannot retain control, and that his achievement is utterly lacking in pleasure or self-fulfillment. Thus, after a series of obscure miscarriages his arrival at an enviable prominence is, ironically, another defeat. The full impact of this blow is graphically illustrated in the final line of the book wherein Ganesh coldly rejects his past, and symbolically his identity: he announces that his new name is G. Ramsay Muir.

The story advances rapidly, Naipaul seldom digressing from a chronological string of events from start to finish. Twelve chapters, a brief epilogue, and internal breaks (both marked and unmarked) subdivide the text into units so that the plot is highly segmented. The gaps, while usually acceptable, are noticeable, and they overemphasize the episodic nature of Naipaul's presentation. The movement, then, frequently jumps ahead from one situation to another, connecting material either left to the reader's imagination or relegated to the narrator for interpolation.

Even though the anonymous narrator is hardly ever present in the body of the story, his occasional direct commentary is still in keeping with the overall fictional scheme of the book. From the outset the plot unfolds within a neatly constructed framework which is held together by the narrator. Chapter One, "The Struggling Masseur," not only gets the story off to a running start by opening *in medias res,* but in conjunction with the appended "Epilogue," it conveniently encloses Ganesh's entire rise and fall.

Had the narrator entered into the action more often than he does, this subtle "framing" effect would probably not have materialized. As it is, he participates at only three points. On the first page he introduces Ganesh at the middle of his career, while the pundit wavers on the border between being an ordinary masseur and becoming the most renowned mystic in the Caribbean. The initial sentence of the book is characteristic of Naipaul's economical style. It sets the perspective in time and creates an anticipatory mood. "Later he was to be famous and honoured throughout the South Caribbean; he was to be a hero of the people and after that, a British representative at Lake Success" (7). Abruptly, without introducing character or speaker, he discloses something of the greatness which yet awaits his hero. With equal conciseness, the remainder of the first page reveals the sardonic humor of the young black boy who serves as narrator, the circumstances which lead to his first meeting Ganesh, and the fact that his story begins at the outbreak of World War II. The remainder of this chapter functions quite normally as a prologue, providing necessary antecedent action, creating certain expectations, and setting the pervasive tone for the rest of the book.

The second point at which the narrator enters as a participating figure comes at the middle of Ganesh's career and fittingly enough just at the center of the novel. The scene which was depicted in the first chapter is here placed in its proper time slot. There is no unnecessary repetition; the speaker simply reflects over the changes in his attitude since the time he visited the now famous masseur. His third active appearance occurs in the epilogue. The time is 1954, the place is a train station in Britain. There is no conclusive evidence, but apparently—since the scene is obviously set after and apart from the body of the story—this last action occurs after the narrator has fairly well established his opinion of the great pundit. At any rate, he is rudely shocked when his enthusiastic reception is coldly rebuffed.

With the clipped phrase and unexpected reversal of events, the history of Ganesh Ramsumair which had seemingly ended is briefly revived only to be shut off as abruptly as it began. There is roughness in this last development as there are awkward points in other parts of the book, but the *Library Journal* reviewer, who argues that the ending is weak, overlooks several mitigating factors.[1] The final conclusion is prepared adequately. Ganesh's disillusionment and hardening come late and without warning, but throughout the novel Naipaul has been subjecting his readers to similarly rapid alterations in movement. The precipitate termination concludes the foregoing narrative quite effectively in that it conforms with what has led up to it.

The surprise ending and some of the other devices used in *The Mystic Masseur* are standard tricks usually eschewed by sophisticated writers. Naipaul skillfully avoids sensationalism in this his first novel, but he is not above the use of mechanical ploys to create suspense, or, more properly, anticipation. The initial sentence of the book may be cited as a successful attempt to elicit expectation. But when the same thing is continually repeated it tends to become monotonous. Another tool seeing extra duty is the ancient "rash promise." Ganesh offhandedly seeks to impress first his prospective father-in-law, next the brash printer, and then his nagging wife by his vague promises to write a book; he overextends himself again in proposing the establishment of a Cultural Institute in obscure Fuente Grove.

Such are the methods Naipaul uses to pull his readers forward.

Insofar as his tools are necessary to continuity and to the sustaining of reader interest, they enhance the novel; it is only when they are employed excessively that they interfere with and weaken the structure.

A major factor mitigating the influence of these minor weaknesses is the type of narrator Naipaul has chosen. The speaker, in whose words events are recorded, has only a brief part in the action. From his numerous bibliographical citations in the text, it appears that most of his knowledge is acquired indirectly, from the books that Ganesh wrote. Reported conversations and intimate private scenes are merely imaginative reconstructions intended to add flesh and color to his account. Reminders of the framework enclosing the biography are subtly woven into the story as the speaker directs attention to significant moments in Ganesh's life.

Nineteen forty-six was the turning-point of Ganesh's career; and as if to underline the fact, in that year he published his autobiography, *The Years of Guilt* (Ganesh Publishing Co. Ltd., Port of Spain. $2.40).
. . . I myself believe that the history of Ganesh is, in a way, the history of our times; and there may be people who will welcome this imperfect account of the man Ganesh Ramsumair, masseur, mystic, and, since 1953, M.B.E. (14)

Similar recurrent interpolations, often shallow and pseudo-intellectual, reveal him to be an ingenuous spokesman. Taking things at face value, using the gift of hindsight, he reflects pretentiously on the portent of insignificant events that later prove to be crucial in the masseur's career. To some extent, it is natural that the expression of such a guileless narrator should have weaknesses. Had Naipaul been more skillful in conceptualizing the role of the narrator or otherwise less obviously dependent on plotting devices, the structure of the first novel would have been greatly strengthened.

As it is, the plot is still a good one. After the preparations of the "prologue" the action moves from one complication to the next until the protagonist overcomes the political crisis in Chapter Ten. Victory and honor are short-lived; almost immediately success turns to alienation at the Governor's dinner and to humiliation in the oil-field riots. These moral defeats would have the mark of tragedy were it not for an ironic twist. While his self-respect slips away, his political fortunes continue to rise. In the "Epilogue" Ganesh's final surrender of principle is exemplified by his anglicization of his Indian name. Thus, the novel is consistent with a viable pattern and is climaxed with a keen satirical thrust.

III   The Suffrage of Elvira

Following the publication of his first book, Naipaul appears not to have been satisfied with his brief sally against the vagaries of politics. He returns to the subject in *The Suffrage of Elvira*. Here he satirizes Trinidad's 1950 election, the first to be held under universal suffrage on the island. Just as Ganesh Ramsumair put up for the 1946 election before, Surujpat "Pat" Harbans now goes up for the Legislative Council. In and near heterogeneous Elvira, a small rural town, there are eight thousand voters—four thousand Hindu, two thousand Negro, one thousand Spanish, and one thousand Muslim. Harbans' only legitimate opponent, Preacher, conducts a quiet walking campaign, going from door to door asking for support. From the start, everyone knows that Harbans' victory is assured; he can count on at least six thousand ballots. The knowledge, however, prevents none of the shrewd operators in Elvira from participating in the exciting new democratic venture.

Again Naipaul's straightforward narrative flows easily within the carefully restrictive limits he has set. A formal prologue and epilogue enclose the thirteen humorously engaging chapters. Internally, an episodic quality persists; transitional passages, a few marred perhaps by the author's overly explicit guiding hand, maintain progression at a quick rate. Naipaul has abandoned the first-person narrator and has assumed an outside position from which to supply necessary exposition. Unfortunately, his artistry is still slightly uneven; there are points, as there are in the first novel, where his technical machinery draws undue attention to itself. The offending passages are few and widely separated, but they are annoyingly inconsistent with Naipaul's best prose. On page 40, while Harbans mulls over discouraging news, the reader is surreptitiously informed, "If he only knew, his troubles hadn't started." Later, when the problems have accumulated, another voice descends from nowhere to second Mrs. Baksh's dire warnings: "She was righter than she knew" (92). The fact that Naipaul can do better than this is witnessed by his deft performance in other places. In many instances he abstains from editorial dictation, allowing essential information to accumulate naturally through characters thinking and interacting within the confines of the dramatic situation. For example, he allows Harbans to worry about the portent of his having struck the dog on his way to Elvira. "But the dog. What about the dog? Where was that going to stall him?" (59). Unobtrusively in his own mind, the superstitious character insinuates that something is to be dreaded in the future; the reader takes the cue from him at this point, not from the author. Little hints like this, signals for upcoming events, occur so frequently that they demand comparison with *The Mystic Masseur*. Naipaul's propensity to stir expectation and cultivate suspense is intensified in his second novel. But here he has not the excuse of the narrator's fictional role; *The Suffrage of Elvira* is constructed on different terms. The action, rather than being presented as the reflections of a biographer, is more immediate; it continually develops from internal cause and effect. Through the emphasis on dramatic presentation, the reader is led to involve himself primarily with character and scene. The illusion is disrupted when extraneous incursions are made.

This issue should not be blown out of proportion, but it reveals a faint touch of immaturity in a promising novel. Viewed as a whole, the structure is executed well enough to render Naipaul's few brief lapses negligible. One cohesive factor running through the book is, as might reasonably be expected, the developing attitude of the political aspirant Harbans. In early meetings with constituents and prospective supporters, his manner is mildly acquiescent, and he is even ashamed of the attention he has drawn. As he submits to one outrageous demand after another, he increasingly distrusts the loyalties of those who are conducting his campaign. His trepidations are, in fact, well founded; their self-interest is quite apparent.

And then Harbans knew. No one in Elvira was fighting *for* him. All Elvira—Preacher, Lorkhoor, Baksh, Chittaranjan, Dhaniram and everybody else—all of them were fighting *him*.

He was nearly seized with another fit of pessimism.
But deep down, despite everything, he knew he was going to win.
He cried and raged; but he wanted to fool, not tempt, fate. (59)

As intrigue thickens and Harbans' voters decline in number from
six thousand to four thousand, his asserted faith undergoes a
severe test. Baksh utilizes the pretext of a family insult from
Chittaranjan to withdraw aid and announce himself as an
opponent in the race.

In spite of each humorously outrageous reversal, Harbans
refuses to give up. As Foam predicts, he overcomes his shyness,
and he learns to suppress his anguish as the money flows out of
his hands. In the final preelection frenzy, however, his acquired
pessimism degenerates into despair: to influence the Negro vote
he has to provide an elaborate funeral for Mr. Cuffy; to regain
the Muslim vote he has to buy back Baksh's loyalty; and on
election eve his hired taxi drivers threaten to strike unless he
writes extra gasoline vouchers. "An [sic] Harbans wrote, and
wrote. If he stopped to think he felt he would break down and
cry. His wrinkled hand perspired and shook; it had never done
so much writing at one time" (211). Harbans wins and his
victory provides a fitting conclusion, but the final climax is
reserved until the epilogue. There the representative of the
people returns to appear before his constituents. Driving a Jaguar,
wearing a double-breasted gray suit, patting his lips with a
freshly ironed handkerchief, and displaying a new cool reserve,
Harbans is just not the candidate they remember. The mob
reaction which develops results in the burning of his new car
and in his furtive ride to safety.

This double ending is reminiscent of the epilogue in *The
Mystic Masseur*, but Naipaul rounds off his second book more
completely by systematically disposing of each of the major
characters in turn. He may have been prompted to this type of
summary because intermingled with the main story there are a
few extra threads that are not sufficiently woven into the plot.
At least two minor subplots are well executed. The childish
rivalry between Foam and Lorkhoor is explicable, and it contributes to the central action. Also, the petty bickering between
Chittaranjan and Ramlogan (a figure obviously carried over
from the first novel) is complete in itself and bears directly on the

election of Harbans. More questionable, however, is the amount of space devoted to Sebastian and to the provocative but unfulfilled suggestion of an affair between Nelly Chittaranjan and Foam. Mahadeo's misadventures with Sebastian are funny, but they are not sufficiently relevant to be treated at such length. As to Nelly's interesting plight as the betrothed bride of an undesirable husband, it almost invites cliché—Foam, the childhood friend, romantically breaking cultural and religious barriers to rescue her at the last moment—but it does not become this trite. And by no means should Naipaul be criticized for avoiding such banality; the objection is that after he begins the line of thought he abandons it. He creates an expectation and fails to fulfill it; and the afterthought of sending Nelly to school abroad, even though it satisfies her daydream, does not compensate for the incomplete development.

Another technical weakness is underscored in the perfunctory last three pages; it has to do with the perspective from which the narrative is presented. Not only has the narrator been removed, but as A. C. Derrick has noted, Naipaul is inconsistent to a noticeable extent in his dramatization of the central character.[2] Since Harbans is supposed to be the major candidate in this election about which the novel is written, it seems logical to assume that his personality would be highly developed; this is not the case. In a majority of instances Harbans and his reactions are described from the outside. Very seldom does he come to life as most of the other characters do. Even the changes in his attitude which mark the successive emotional stages of plot development come largely from external observation. He is seldom allowed to act or speak for himself, and as a result he never really becomes essential to the action.

In *The Suffrage of Elvira* Naipaul is still experimenting with form. With the addition of minor subplots he has slightly increased the depth and complexity of his expression. Detrimental to his work up to this point, however, is his failure to maintain a consistent quality of internal control. Separate episodes are fairly well integrated into the structure, and the characters with which he succeeds—in most cases the more colorful the better—are well done. What problem exists with prolonged consistency is over-

shadowed by the effects of his felicitous handling, within carefully
restricted limits, of such a variety of characters and actions.

IV   Miguel Street

Appearing next in order of publication is the book which
is actually the first one written by Naipaul. Treatment of *Miguel
Street* has been reserved until now because even though it was
conceived first, it was withheld by the author until he was
apparently satisfied as to its completeness. Even more than the
second and third novels, this work reflects the color and texture
of Caribbean life. Whereas the others center primarily on professional figures—a masseur and a politician—*Miguel Street* delves
into the lower strata of Trinidad society. As the title implies,
it deals with the people of the street, the men and women who
meet and live together there on intimate terms with poverty and
frustrating meaninglessness.

The story is recounted from memories of the narrator's early
island life before he "secures" a scholarship to study abroad. In
looking back on his youth, he makes an attempt to recapture the
salient features of the people who influenced his most impression-
able years. The result is a curiously poignant mixture of humor
and pathos. Residents and transients on his out-of-the-way street
would appear to be a faceless mob to an outsider, but to him they
constitute a world.

A stranger could drive through Miguel Street and just say "Slum!"
because he could see no more. But we who lived there saw our
street as a world, where everybody was quite different from everybody else. Man-Man was mad; George was stupid; Big Foot was
a bully; Hat was an adventurer; Popo was a philosopher; and Morgan
was our comedian. (79)

This summary occurs almost halfway through the book, after
the reader has already seen how the particular labels fit the
men they describe.

Each chapter dwells upon one character and his particular
problem or aspiration. The first three chapters are concerned
with marital difficulties. Bogart's bigamy is caused by his desire
for peer approval, or as Hat expresses it he runs away from his
women, "To be a man, among we men" (16). George abuses his

wife until she dies, his daughter until she marries, and his son until the child outgrows him; and then he dies, looking "old, and weary, and very sad" (35). His son Elias is so afraid of tests that he never realizes his dream of escape through scholarship. He becomes a garbage collector. Chapters Five through Nine play variations on similar themes of personal failure. Man-Man is committed to an asylum after he acts out a crucifixion in the nearby hills. B. (for Black) Wordsworth wants to write the greatest poem in the world, and for a while he makes the drabness of the narrator's reality come alive with wonder and beauty. On his deathbed he confesses that all his romantic schemes were lies. George, the practical joker who enjoys making fun of himself, is crushed when others really laugh at him.

In the midst of the depression of these lives there is an indomitable spirit which keeps breaking to the surface. The narrator's uncle Bhakcu sets a valuable example for his nephew: absurd as his life is, he finds enjoyment in living. "The men in the street didn't like Bhakcu because they considered him a nuisance. But I liked him for the same reason that I liked Popo, the carpenter. For, thinking about it now, Bhakcu was also an artist. He interfered with motor-cars for the joy of the thing, and he never seemed worried about money" (157). Hat is like that too, at first—until he gets married. His wife is unfaithful, however, and he is sentenced to four years in prison for beating her almost to death. The boy is fifteen when Hat, the man whose wry aphorisms have provided terms by which he has learned to grasp reality, begins to serve his sentence. When he is released he finds that at eighteen the boy has outgrown adolescence.

The final chapter brings the young narrator into contact with the famed Ganesh. It is through the former mystic that the necessary bribes secure a scholarship which will enable the narrator to leave the island for study abroad. Thus through education, the dream that eludes his friend Elias, he is permitted to extract himself from the futile existence of Miguel Street. His parting from his mother and uncle Bhakcu brings the book to an especially appropriate close.

I embraced my mother.
I said to Bhakcu, "Uncle Bhak, I didn't want to tell you before, but I think I hear your tappet knocking."

His eyes shone.

I left them all and walked briskly towards the aeroplane, not
looking back, looking only at my shadow before me, a dancing
dwarf on the tarmac. (222)

The decorum of this passage speaks for itself, and the bittersweet
mockery of the topical jest epitomizes the tone of the entire
novel—terse, aware, and deeply human.

Episodes in this novel are not bound together as self-consciously as they were in the earlier published works, but the
underlying structure may be Naipaul's most consistent yet.
He again resorts to an ingenuous speaker to shape the reader's
response. In *Miguel Street*, unlike *The Mystic Masseur*, he goes
one step farther and provides a second character to serve as a
foil· to the naïveté of the primary commentator. The result is a
more evenly balanced perspective, and it effectively conceals
the author's controlling hand. As in *The Mystic Masseur*, the narrator speaks of the action in the past tense. In his review he is
careful to preserve the normal immaturity that marks the first
eighteen years of his life. Emendations to his first impressions
follow quite naturally since he should have gained in experience
and knowledge at the time he looks back.

Hat's contribution to the structure is a crucial one. In his role
as the shrewd observer and formulator of maxims, he broadens
the narrative's perspective. It would not have been in character
for the young speaker to understand the deeper significance of
the reality in which he was embroiled, and his constant references to Hat's responses indicate the main source of his earliest
psychological awakenings. The importance of the narrator's
expanding awareness is what makes *Miguel Street* fit the pattern of the *Bildungsroman*. Since the story is presented as past
action, however, the process of thought development is not
emphasized. Instead, the narrator provides an edited survey
of his childhood. The youngster's growth is shown, but it is
accomplished more by revealing his accumulated experiences
than by tracing out a systematic development.

A carefully regulated growth pattern might have been
pleasantly neat for fiction, but it could have also been artificial,
and *Miguel Street* is better for its more subtly unified structure.
There are seventeen characters including the narrator and Hat,

who are each given separate chapters to themselves in addition to scattered references throughout the book. The movement through these individuals tends to lead from the particular to the general. This should not be taken to mean that the personalities become less specifically identified but that later chapters bring increasingly wider horizons. From Bogart to B. Wordsworth the action is limited to local eccentrics who fail to get outside themselves. B. Wordsworth ends up admitting that his life is a falsehood, but not before he has interested the young boy in the beauty and depth of natural nature. Two more chapters on limited figures intervene, and then Titus Hoyt opens the door (with mixed results) to journalism, literature, foreign languages, and world affairs.

"The Maternal Instinct" through "The Mechanical Genius" focus on two social institutions, the family unit and the municipal sanitation department. Laura, the mother of eight illegitimate children by seven different men, and Mrs. Hereira, who has deserted a rich husband to live with a man who beats her, point up two examples of the domestic chaos of Miguel Street. Located somewhere between these extremes is the narrator's own home life, which in these pages begins to emerge more clearly. In part, his attachment for Hat and his uncle Bhakcu may be explained by the fact that he has no father. His mother manages to clothe and feed him, but for male companionship and guidance he must take to the street. On the street, the scale of values is clearly not very high. Eddoes, Elias, and most of his friends, despairing of achieving wider distinction, aspire to grow up to be garbage cart drivers. The driver's blue cart, distinctive uniform, and connection with civil government appear to be highly desirable in this restrictive environment.

The wider world makes significant invasions from Chapter Fourteen on. In this chapter Bolo finally accepts the news that World War II has ended, and in Chapter Fifteen the presence of the American base on the island brings more outside influence to bear on the street. In the chapter entitled "Hat" the boy at last arrives at maturity. Hat, who has substituted as a father figure, is taken to prison, and when he is released three years later, his eighteen-year-old protégé has grown beyond him.

A long time. But it was just three years, three years in which
I had grown up and looked critically at the people around me. I no
longer wanted to be like Eddoes. He was so weak and thin, and
I hadn't realised that he was so small. Titus Hoyt was stupid and
boring, and not funny at all. Everything had changed.
When Hat went to jail, part of me had died. (213-14)

What has died, of course, is his childhood. His apprenticeship
served, all that remains is his departure as a man into the world.
Thus it is that the narrator's expanding horizons shape the skeletal
structure of *Miguel Street*.

An intriguing study remains to be made of the original and
the final manuscripts of this novel. If major changes are discovered—and if the first two published works are any indication of his early style—Naipaul's experimentation and practice
in narrative techniques have been profitable. Either that, or all
along Naipaul was creating in *Miguel Street* better than he knew.
Advantageous to this novel is the consistent immediacy of the
point of view from which the narrative is presented, and the
substitution of less obtrusive double spacing for the editorial
stars. At least for the present, he has foregone anticipatory
devices, and his abrupt turns are made more palatable by his
working them more integrally into the scenes in which they
occur. His work is still episodic, and *Miguel Street* is more a
collection of overlapping and interconnected sketches than a
standard novel, but other considerations aside, with the noticeable
refinements in his structural machinery, he has laid a solid
foundation for his mature fiction.

V   A House for Mr Biswas

With the appearance in 1961 of *A House for Mr Biswas*,
Naipaul may have published his best fiction. It is even possible
that this book is the best novel yet to emerge from the Caribbean.
It is a vital embodiment of authentic West Indian life, but more
than that, it transcends national boundaries and evokes universal
human experiences. Mr. Biswas' desire to own his own house is
essentially a struggle to assert personal identity and to attain
security—thoroughly human needs.

From the evil omens of his birth to his debt-surrounded death in middle age, Mr. Biswas' life consists of one misfortune after another. Physically inadequate for field work, he has to be put to school. With the accidental death of his father (caused by Biswas), the family breaks up, and he begins his life of moves from one house of strangers to another. His education terminates on the whim of an aunt, and, unprepared for any profession, he trains and fails as a pundit, then drifts into work as an itinerant painter of signs. While following this trade he almost inadvertently marries into the stultifying Tulsi family. Time and again he is driven in disgust from the oppressive Tulsis to seek a living. In Port of Spain he finally achieves a modicum of success as a reporter for the *Trinidad Sentinel*. Through this job he manages to move up to work briefly in a short-lived governmental department. With the elimination of the department, he must take a cut in salary and return to the *Trinidad Sentinel* where he works until ten weeks before his death.

The culmination of Mr. Biswas' problems comes in his purchase of a makeshift house on Sikkim Street. Burdened with debt and worried about the future of his family, he ruins his health, loses his job, and is reduced to living on his daughter's salary. But at this nadir of his life, he discovers in the depth of his being a surprisingly resilient spirit. Writing to his son, who has refused to correspond with him, he begins to expound upon the unexpected delights that he finds all around him in simple things: his daughter's faithfulness, rides in the car, flowers, and the pleasant shade of his favorite tree. His death, like his life, is unexciting; the funeral is announced in the papers and over the radio, and mourners pour in to pay their respects. "The polished floor became scratched and dusty; the staircase shivered continually; the top floor resounded with the steady shuffle. And the house did not fall" (531).

As in *The Mystic Masseur* Naipaul reveals the end of the story before it begins, denying himself whatever superficial value might have resided in the temptation to keep the reader in suspense as to what would happen to his hero. The first chapter and the epilogue again serve as "frames" for the plot, enclosing the shifting scenery of Mr. Biswas' world. From the early novels Naipaul retains anticipatory and summary passages, to a lesser degree minor unmarked breaks and mild shifts in narrative direc-

tion, and a few brief looks into the future; but these are now made
so integral to the action of the story that they are unobtrusive,
no longer drawing attention to themselves as plotting devices.
As a matter of fact, on each level of the novel the structure is consistently molded more and more deeply into the texture of
meaning. A. C. Derrick assesses the density of this novel's
layered structure.

The framework of the novel is clearly significant. The careful
structure of Prologue, Swelling Act and Epilogue; the formal,
chronological build-up of Biswas's character; the thematic design
of imagery and symbol, all conspire, in a purely artistic appeal to
the imagination, to produce a pervasive contrasting backdrop to
Biswas's quest for form. Furthermore, the even, deliberate structure
of the novel, with the recurring images of darkness, decay and
death, makes failure appear throughout as the inevitable outcome
to the process of Biswas's struggle.[3]

As Derrick notes, on one level the framework is almost an outline, on a second it is a developing portrait, on a third it is an
informing backdrop, and on another it is a fusion of motifs and
themes.

Episodic as usual, the forthright plot of this finely wound
novel does not separate easily into its several aspects, nor can the
plot be divided from other aspects of the book. Even to its inter-
spersed patterns of symbols and motifs, the narrative is connected
with everything else. "Naipaul's calculated simplicity should not
obscure from us the fact that many of the novel's most telling
effects are obtained by employing a consistent structure of
imagery and near-symbolism which operates on the surface of the
novel but which gives a consistency and immediacy to what
would otherwise be a disorganized and rambling narrative."[4]
As should be the case with the best fiction, to unfold the pattern
of emotional development is essentially to analyze characterization, and to explore narrative technique is to investigate the
texture of language throughout the work. Naipaul abandons
narrative persona and simply concentrates on the presentation of
an intriguing story. Technically, he employs the omniscient narrator, but the relation progresses with such unobtrusive ease
that the reader's attention is seldom, if ever, distracted from the
evolving action. About the closest to a breakdown in the point of

view, as noted by Kenneth Ramchand, is the author's overly insistent denunciation of the Tulsi style of living both in direct statement and accumulated imagery.[5]

Critical moments in Mr. Biswas' life serve to point up the growth in his personality from the passivity of youth and early manhood to a more active participation in the shaping of events. He never exerts control, but he does become more and more assertive in his limited way. Early events such as his haphazard marriage and his ineffectual attempts to escape the Tulsis at The Chase and at Green Vale underscore the negativity of his attitude. The responsibilities that accompany his adventures into freedom are more than he can bear. As a result, the disastrous pressures that overwhelm him at Green Vale teach him the value of surrender and acceptance. "Lying in the room next to Shama's, perpetually dark, Mr Biswas slept and woke and slept again. The darkness, the silence, the absence of the world enveloped and comforted him. At some far-off time he had suffered great anguish. He had fought against it. Now he had surrendered, and his surrender had brought peace" (269). The respite is temporary, but at this point, the conclusion of Part One of the book, Mr. Biswas reviews his situation and realizes that "Green Vale had given him an experience of unhappiness against which everything had now to be measured" (273). He accepts the tenuous security of the Tulsi house for his family and gathers enough confidence in himself to go out into the world, "to test it for its power to frighten" (274).

His confidence wanes almost immediately in Part Two, but he begins to act more positively, not just escaping, but moving toward goals—minor in themselves and unimpressive by most standards—but positive ones. He literally clowns his way into employment by the *Trinidad Sentinel*. At Shorthills, with calculation, he slowly works at securing his personal integrity. "For him Shorthills was an adventure, an interlude. His job made him independent of the Tulsis; and Shorthills was an insurance against the sack" (363). Eventually he achieves temporary victories: the change in jobs from reporter to welfare worker, and if not in the purchase of the poorly constructed house on Sikkim Street, at least in his decisive reaction against being duped by the seller into giving up part of his property. None of

his actions are large ones, and it is the beauty of the book
that Naipaul has succeeded in making the biography of such an
inconsequential hero into the intriguing narrative that it is.

Structurally, *A House for Mr Biswas* is remarkably sound.
The rising action reaches an effective climax with the emotional
breakdown and recovery in Part One; on the second plateau
the movement accelerates smoothly and culminates in an
appropriately higher climax in the final pages of Part Two.
The power of the narrative derives largely from the con-
vincing inevitability of the plot. The only point at which
belief is strained is in the sudden appearance of a buyer for the
abandoned house at Shorthills. This *deus ex machina* allows Mr.
Biswas to purchase his final home at a time when he had
apparently reached an impasse with the Tulsi household. The
false note is made more acceptable, however, when it leads
ironically to a pyrrhic victory. The Sikkim Street move is, after
all, a very dubious improvement. But the final realization of
another absurd mistake, and the acceptance of good and evil
complete the pattern of Mr. Biswas' story. Theme, character,
and plot merge in the conclusion, giving Naipaul's fourth novel
the full effectiveness of the best traditional fiction.

VI   Mr Stone and the Knights Companion

Thus far, *A House for Mr Biswas* has been Naipaul's last
exclusively West Indian novel. Those coming after it have shifted
in locality and/or in the nationality of characters. *Mr Stone and
the Knights Companion* is a complete break with the Caribbean.
Mr. Stone is thoroughly British, and his only contact with the
colonies is second-handed, through his wife's pictures and furnish-
ings—mementos left over from her deceased first husband's former
visit to India. This major change in setting is the most obvious,
but not the only difference, between this and the last book: the
"framing" technique disappears entirely; chapter titles are omit-
ted; the field of action is severely restricted; and the tightly-knit
story is told in less than 160 pages.

Mr. Stone's waning years before retirement are recounted dis-
passionately and with the liquid ease that is typical of Naipaul's
style. The plot flows smoothly in unadulterated simplicity from

one brief episode into the next. The incident with the cat that frightens Mr. Stone on the opening page becomes the subject of a personal joke on himself at a party soon afterward. At the party he is drawn by the sympathetic laughter and interest of Mrs. Springer into a friendship that blossoms and later results in their marriage. The marriage occurs shortly before the time Mr. Stone reaches the age of mandatory retirement and is at least in part a reaction against his growing insecurity. His sensitivity over the prospect of retirement increases, and his wife's solicitous behavior reaches deeper into his emotions until he is depressed and revolted by the prospect of a useless old age of inactivity. Seeing the recently retired man at Miss Chichester's teashop drives him in desperation to seek to provide a stay against the encroaching emptiness. The outcome of his feverish thinking and writing is the scheme for the "Knights Companion," a program to provide activity and companionship for elderly employees who have been released by the firm for which Mr. Stone works. His program assumes its own momentum and to his chagrin soon leaves him in its wake. Youthful men pass over him; he is dejected by his loss of importance; his close friend Tony dies; and as another spring begins to emerge he focuses his attention again on the black cat. " 'They're having it destroyed,' Margaret said. 'Mrs Midgeley was telling me' " (140). From this point on Mr. Stone is obsessed with the cat, who, like him, is awaiting extinction.

As things fall apart, Mr. Stone reaches the conclusion that he was wrong to have attempted to organize his life by creative activity. "The order of the universe, to which he had sought to ally himself, was not his order. So much he had seen before. But now he saw, too, that it was not by creation that man demonstrated his power and defied this hostile order, but by destruction" (158-59). His reflections on man's destructive capabilities are rudely shattered when, in the same hallway where he had first been attacked by the old cat, he is again frightened by a cat, the lively offspring of his original enemy. After the initial shock, "fear blended into guilt, guilt into love" (159), and the segment of his life that we have been admitted to view has run full circle. Mr. Stone is not, however, simply returned to where he began; he has profited by his recent experiences. He has

learned that he is no destroyer, that even though his familiar
world has collapsed about him he has survived, and further, he
knows that calm will return and that life, sometimes empty and
lonely, continues.

In effect, the emotional patterning of this short book is cir-
cular. The revolving seasons, the recurring identifications with
the tree and the cat, and the cyclical hope and disillusionment
of Mr. Stone as he observes his fate in that of others all contribute to the circularity. Mr. Stone desires continuity; looking
back, he is amazed at the order of his life, but viewing the
uncertain future frightens him. Though his arrangements are
briefly shaken by his late change from bachelorhood, he manages to adjust and again falls into routine. But as he observes
the serenity of the tree outside his window and his diminishing
hostility toward the cat, he senses the loss of something from
his world, and time begins to speed by him.

The tree, changing, developing with the year, made its point
every day. And when, sitting at the Sunday tea, trying to reassure
himself by his precise, neat, slow gestures, he sometimes said, "You
are part of me, Margaret. I don't know what I would do without
you," he spoke with an urgency and gratitude she did not fully
understand. (59)

What he has lost is his feeling of order and permanence; his life
is passing by, and he needs something to insure against confusion and destruction.

Two important scenes turn the narrative so that it curves upon
itself. Following closely upon his disorientation in the fields
near Chysauster, he reluctantly witnesses what he is likely to
become in retirement. This prompts the burst of energy that
results in the plan for the Knights Companion, but built into
the scheme are the elements of disillusionment that overwhelm
him when another worker gets all the credit for his idea. The
second scene centers around the desolation after Bill Whymper
steals his bid for recognition and a place in the world's memory.
At the end of Chapter Six he has descended below the emotional
letdown experienced at Miss Chichester's. Here his thoughts turn
to destruction and chaos; that is, until he encounters the young
cat. What he seems to realize in the conclusion is that there is

continuity, there is renewal, life does go on even if private worlds collapse and individuals are forgotten. The crises, though minor in scale, are traumatic periods in his life, and their resolution culminates his experience and satisfies the expectations created in the narrative.

It is characteristic of Naipaul's later fiction that expectation and scope and intensity of action become more and more reduced. In *Mr Stone and the Knights Companion*, for example, even though an omniscient author presides over development, the central character is already mature and settled in his personality, and all that takes place is his painful adjustment to the inevitable problems (primarily emotional and mental) of old age. Naipaul has continually avoided sensationalism and melodramatic outbursts, but after *A House for Mr Biswas* the events he portrays are increasingly subdued in tone. In fact, a majority of the activity portrayed is internalized, given the form of mental reflection rather than of physical participation; and the shift in emphasis results in significant structural changes.

VII   The Mimic Men

The Mimic Men is Naipaul's third novel on colonial politics, and it is by far his most complex and bitter treatment of the subject. The basic framework is, in fact, an improved replica of that employed in *The Mystic Masseur*. This time Naipaul's now familiar chronicle technique takes the form of a deposed office-holder's autobiography. Complicating the plot is the fact that events are not revealed in chronological order. Instead, it is up to the reader to arrange and fill in time slots as antecedent material is supplied during the course of the shifting narrative. Ranjit "Ralph" Kripal Singh (whose name is not mentioned before page 111) was born and raised on the island of Isabella. Early experiences at school and among his family and friends are of such a tenuous nature (they leave him with such insecurity and instability) that he often imagines he is shipwrecked and stranded on a desert island at the end of the world. In another of his fantasies he is an Aryan chieftain leading his horsemen through the snow-clad high passes of romantically distant mountains. His father "Gurudeva" contributes both to his fantasy and his embarrassment by breaking with society and establishing a mendicant community in the rural hills. Ralph sees his father and himself as chieftains without kingdoms, leaders absurdly marked by fate and then forgotten.

Oddly enough, Gurudeva's infamy paves the way for Ralph's political future; it focuses attention on him. His mother's family already has wealth, and Ralph is capable of making his own money, but in the emerging movement toward island nationalism it is his blood relationship with a popular activist that finally thrusts him forward. Even before he leaves the island for study abroad, his childhood friends look to him as special; but the pressures make his school days miserable. The grotesque horse sacrifice, the *Asvamedha*, attributed to his father as an act of political defiance, taints his ideals and confirms his determination to escape.

Withdrawal: it became urgent now for me. Before it had been part of fantasy, part of the urge to escape shipwreck and return to lands I had fashioned in my imagination, lands of horsemen, high plains, mountains and snow; and time had been as unreal as place. Now I felt the need only to get away, to a place unknown, among people whose lives and even language I need never enter. (173-74)

His escape is made to school in England, where after many days of forlorn wandering about the cold city and among "two-dimensional" people, he accidentally meets Sandra. Their mutual aimlessness and despair draw them together in spite of racial and cultural differences—he is colonial Indian, she is metropolitan white—and marriage follows. Plans are changed, and they return to Isabella where they join the island's sophisticated, vacuous nouveau riche. From the start, Ralph reveals an infallible talent for profitable land investment and real estate development. The money accumulates; power comes to his hand; but as he succeeds in business, his personal life simultaneously degenerates.

Almost out of a reaction against boredom he allows his old classmate Browne to involve him, first in editing a socialistic periodical, and then in supporting a campaign for political office. Running on a platform of independent home rule, Browne leads him and their followers in a frenzied race toward a goal that none of them comprehends. Success comes, but with it also comes unavoidable recognition that they have overreached themselves. "From this awareness of weakness—strength only when it was in combat with something we judged to be strong— we arrived at dismay.... It has happened in twenty countries like ours: the sobering moment of success, when playacting turns out to be serious" (240). Since their program has been one of opposition, as they discover with the removal of obstacles, they really have no program at all. The realization epitomizes the falsity and emptiness that have plagued Ralph all his life. He and his colleagues are mimic men; they play roles that are meaningless.

After his wife leaves him, his friends desert, and "crunch-time" deprives him of influence and his position, he secludes himself at the age of forty in a quiet old hotel in London.

It does not worry me now, as it worried me when I began this book [Ralph writes], that at the age of forty I should find myself at the end of my active life. I do not now think this is even true. I no longer yearn for ideal landscapes... I have lived through attach- ment and freed myself from one cycle of events. It gives me joy to find that in so doing I have also fulfilled the fourfold division of life prescribed by our Aryan ancestors. I have been student, house- holder and man of affairs, recluse. (300)

According to his own thinking, he is regrouping his forces, fearing action, but preparing himself to take up another task, this time unemotionally and without distracting complications. This approach cannot succeed, of course, for a human being with normal feelings. Apparently, though, his plan is not to engage again in life; he is going to view human attachments in paren- thesis and set his own existence in a separate realm. "So writing, for all its initial distortion, clarifies, and even becomes a process of life" (301).

This is unquestionably one of the most negative endings at which Naipaul has yet arrived. The protagonist asserts his will to continue, but the existence he envisions for himself is a barren void—no love, no hope, no ideals, none of the spiritual or emotional essentials that make a human being more than an automaton. This conclusion, however, does not make the book itself negative, nor does it shut the valves of feeling too exclusively. In view of the internal principles upon which the novel is constructed, it seems that those critics are wrong who condemn Naipaul for being too academic in his presentation and (in a related criticism) for restricting the point of view to an egotistical, narrow-minded narrator.[6]

If the basic framework of the novel is kept clearly in mind and the narrator's voice is not confused with the author's, these objections can be satisfactorily resolved. The narrative is delivered, as it is in *The Mystic Masseur*, from a retrospective position. Because the speaker has at the age of forty attained a stable, relatively emotionless state, it is easy to accept the static quality of his story; the detached reserve of his voice is in keeping with the hypothetical situation of the fictional creation. The narrator, like him or not, is established in personality from the beginning; we do not observe his process of development, but his rationalizations for the life he has already lived. A. C. Derrick apparently misses this point in the following judgment of the novel: "Too much of it fails to go beyond mere verbal statement, for though the narrative asserts that Isabella is a second-hand colony of uncreative men . . . where society is fragmented and inorganic, exhausted, fraudulent and cruel, there is hardly enough concrete demonstration of such qualities."[7] On the contrary, the lack of concreteness, the loss of reality, is precisely the point of the book. The mimic men, of whom the narrator is representative, live a fantasy existence; they assume roles, and even while they are aware of the discrepancy they attempt to live as though reality were what they pretend it is. These men are apparently exhausted by the absurdity that plagues them; like men of the "lost generation" their sensitivity to man's inability to realize the ideals that loom just beyond reach has made them cynical and self-destructive. Ralph Singh's static attitude of resignation becomes ever more dominant as his peculiar interpretation of the past builds up to his final escape into obscurity.

Unless the narrator is accepted along with his personal idiosyncrasies, the carefully sustained fabric of *The Mimic Men* will be misunderstood. He is egotistical, selfishly introverted and detached, and he seldom allows alternative concepts to enter into his narrative. Admittedly, this severely limits the scope of the book and sets it one remove from the type of dramatic tension which might normally be preferred, but the chosen method is exonerated by one overriding virtue—it consistently answers to the design of the novel. To ask Naipaul to do other than he has done is to ask him to write a different book.

Naipaul is better able to sustain his own detachment and the point of view of his protagonist in *The Mimic Men* than he is in *The Mystic Masseur*. His advantage in the later novel is that the "framing" is less obtrusive, and the narrator's participation in the story proper is more conveniently explicable. Ralph Singh is, after all, telling his own story, while the black boy has to drag in Ganesh's writings to support his authenticity. Ralph's frequent philosophical incursions into the text are natural outgrowths of the fact that he is simultaneously inside and outside of the action; he shows himself performing, and then he pauses to comment on his performance. "I cannot speak of the [political] movement as a phenomenon generated by my personality. I can scarcely speak of it in personal terms. The politician deals in abstractions, even when he deals with himself. He is a man lifted out of himself and separate from his personality, which he might acknowledge from time to time" (230). The concept of the artist editing himself is unavoidable with the frequent references to mimicry, playacting, drama, film, and the "celestial camera" which "recorded my every movement, impartially, without judgment or pity" (114). With hindsight, this development in Naipaul's technique might almost appear to be predictable. Each of his novels (with the qualified exception, perhaps, of *Mr Stone and the Knights Companion*) has been carefully placed within a frame which effectively separates it from outside reality. The frame is not necessarily artificial, but it reminds the reader more or less subconsciously of the presence of the artist-creator, until now in *The Mimic Men* the very presence of the narrator himself has developed into one of the primary focal points of the novel.

With these preliminary observations about the narrative voice in mind, the approach to the intricate structure of this novel is facilitated. Naipaul uses, as a *Times Literary Supplement* reviewer terms it, what is not so much a flashback as a "dissolving" technique.[8] Not only episodes, but huge sections of *The Mimic Men* are taken out of chronological order and related according to the sequence imposed by the narrator's wandering

memories. The manipulations of time are handled with such
ease—what with moods and images carried back and forth—that
continuity never falters; and the fluctuating dreaminess of the
narrator's mental state only adds to the blending and mixing
of realism and fantasy.

Of the three constituent parts of the book, Part One is especially marked by time shifts: in the first three pages, the speaker
recalls a period from his first visit to London; for the next four
pages he jumps to his present mood, which resembles that of the
period he has just remembered; then for twenty-four pages he
resumes where he had left off in the past and carries up to his
marriage and his first return trip to Isabella. Another break
for the present and eleven pages of conjecture, and then the
meeting with Sandra, their marriage and life together on the
island is told. The concluding chapter, one paragraph in length,
is set in the present, a candid discussion of his "instinct" for
having undertaken his own history.

Part Two is comparatively simple in outline. It merely traces
the protagonist's early years from childhood through his coming
of age and first departure from the island. It is significant that
this part should be the most dramatically portrayed in the novel.
The secondary characters are depicted more fully, and action
is carried out more extensively. The reason for this may be that
Ralph Singh's childhood seems more vivid to him than the
increasingly false existence that grows upon him as he drifts
further and further from his shallowly rooted island boyhood.
This part also ends with a single-paragraph chapter of reflection.
Here, though, he broods over the news of the death of his father
and is remembering how his desolation had driven him to Sandra.
The final part of the book reiterates the political intrigue that
undermines his friendships, his home, his fortune, and leads
to his exile in England. After an affair in London, he returns
once to Isabella to verify the fact that his past is now closed
to him forever, and in the final pages he sets his philosophical
house in order.

In dramatic terms, each of the three parts builds to a minor
crisis, and in a sense each might stand alone as a short story.
There is, however, a basic incompleteness that makes the three
parts interdependent. Expectations created in the first section

are left unexplained until the narrative reaches points deeply embedded in later passages; the childhood sequences lead up to events that occur in the last division. Throughout the story, threads are meticulously dropped and picked up again at well-chosen intervals, so that up to the last moment the segments of the past are being woven into the emerging fabric. In design, unlike that of his previous novels, the ending of *The Mimic Men* is highly inconclusive. No one, least of all the narrator himself, knows where his life will lead henceforth. The open-endedness of this plot is quite a concession to modernism on the part of Naipaul, who in many ways so often follows conventions of the traditional Victorian novel.

VIII   A Flag on the Island

A Flag on the Island is the title novelette in a collection of short stories and sketches. Though written as early as 1965 (two years before *The Mimic Men*), it was withheld from publication until 1967. A case could be made for placing it before, yet for several important reasons (which will be introduced below), it seems more appropriate to handle it as later than *The Mimic Men*. It is only eighty-seven pages in length, but its brevity belies the wealth of material that is concisely packed into those few pages. Naipaul returns in setting and in most of his characters to the islands of the Caribbean, but as is typical of his later novels, he continues to generate a more cosmopolitan atmosphere; this time he adopts a protagonist from the outside world, an American. The plot is not as involved as that in *The Mimic Men*, but the thin line between reality and unreality is maintained to such an extent that there is surprising complexity and depth in the simple narrative.

Frank (whose surname is never given), along with everyone else aboard his tourist liner, is forced by Hurricane Irene to harbor at the West Indian island where he had been stationed during World War II. Because of enduringly painful emotional entanglements which remain from his former stay on the island, he is reluctant to risk venturing on land. When he does go ashore, as he has feared, he is unable to resist the temptation to stir up old troubles by reestablishing contact with his neglected

friends. His roots in the past weigh heavily enough on him, but
added to this burden is his unavoidable confirmation of the
onerous changes that have corrupted the island "paradise." In
effect the story—action internalized for the most part, in keeping
with the trend of the late novels—is a stream-of-consciousness
account of the narrator's absorption of the shocking alterations
that have occurred in his absence. Henry, his boon companion
and freewheeling adviser in the mores of island life, has dwindled
under his wife's shrewish direction into a prosperous but miserably unhappy nightclub proprietor. Priest, an itinerate seer and
unfortunate insurance salesman, is reduced, under the name of
Gary Priestland, to the role of a television personality. J. J.
Blackwhite, would-be author and defender of the arts, still
struggling with an overwhelming identity problem, has developed
into an ethnic culture-monger and coy baiter of wealthy foundations. But the deepest cut of all is the change in Selma, the
mistress he had left behind, now living with Gary Priestland in
a suburban bungalow with all the modern accouterments that
standardize it into hackneyed cliché.

Depressed and sickened by the transformations that surround
him, Frank almost lapses into helpless despair. What revives
him is the suddenly inspiring thought that the approaching hurricane might wipe the slate clean, might purify everything by
destroying it.

Selma, be weak like me. Henry is right. Priest is right. It is all
going to be laid flat. Let us rejoice. Let us go to the bay. Let us
take Henry with us. And afterwards, if there is an afterwards, Henry
will take us to his pretty little island.
There are no more islands. It's not you talking. It's the wind. (230)

Of course, Selma is correct; there is no respite, no escape from
reality, and she recognizes the irrationality of his desperation.
But a frenzy has possessed him, and his staccato expression of
feeling indicates the pressure that is building within his mind.
The hurricane does shatter the monotony and break people out
of their molds—briefly—but as soon as the crisis passes the shadow
of conformity returns, and Frank is back where he started at
the first of the story. "And in the city where each exhausted
person had once more to accommodate himself to his fate, to

the life that had not been arrested, I went back to the hotel" (235). Thus another of Naipaul's novels runs full circle, beginning with an established mood, going back to the informing sources of the mood, carrying them through to the height of intensity, and then returning in the end to confirm the existing status.

Dramatically climaxing *A Flag on the Island* is an obvious *danse macabre*. "The world was ending and the cries that greeted this end were cries of joy. We all began to dance. We saw dances such as we had seen in the old days in Henry's yard. No picking of cotton, no cutting of cane; no carrying of water, no orchestrated wails. We danced with earnestness" (232). Considering the darkening mood that pervades the recent books, this apocalyptic turn seems appropriate not only for the climax of *A Flag on the Island* but for all the preceding novels. Mr. Stone is too old to begin again, but indications are that he would have been able and willing to go on if he could. Ralph Singh, on the other hand, needs more than the opportunity of a fresh start; he apparently lacks the will to resume life. Coming after these, Frank seems to have gone beyond the point of return; nothing short of cataclysmic obliteration will wash the banality out of his existence. A somber mood, perhaps a dead end—but Naipaul does not leave it at that. The quotidian ensues as it always has in life and as it has in all his fiction.

The emotional pattern does not develop to any great extent in this story; the movement is more one of intensification. As several of the characters indicate, Frank is well known for his "moods." His dominant mood changes only in the direction of increased fervor. As in the other novels, then, the basic structure hinges upon the personality of a limited narrator. Readers see through his eyes and feel through his emotions.

The narrator's voice is so consistently in control that in this story the author's hand never appears. Unless an attempt is made to read Naipaul's direct statements from other works into the narrator's perspective, the fictional veil is not disturbed; there is certainly nothing in the text to disrupt the "suspension of disbelief." Even for an explanation of the comically tag-named characters, Chippy, Bippy, and Tippy, it is necessary to look no further than the humorous bent of Frank's mind. When he sees

foolish men pursuing a silly impostor, he allows his cynical fancy
to consume them and then presents his subjective conceptualization. The same goes for Priest's maddened preaching before the
imminent storm; any exaggeration or distortion of actuality is
attributable to the clearly defined personality of a highly agi-
tated narrator. The stream of consciousness freely intermingles
inner and outer realities to produce a variable perspective which
one critic has described as jagged and hallucinatory in style.[9]
This fanciful element perhaps more than anything else accounts
for the story's subtitle—*A Fantasy for a Small Screen.* Whether
or not the script was really ever intended for a movie, as Naipaul
contends in his preface, the fantasy is in a sense projected on
the pages of his shortest novel. The screen is small, but the
picture is in clear, vivid color.

IX   In a Free State

The scenario of the title novella in *In a Free State* is similarly
limited in scope. Narrative tone of voice and perspective never
falter, and with a minimum of structural machinery the simple
plot unfolds naturally. The main characters are introduced—
Bobby, a homosexual Englishman who is assisting the development of home rule for a new African nation, and Linda, the
"man-eating" wife of another expatriate Englishman—then the
narrative follows as these two motor from the country's northern
capital to their home in the Southern Collectorate. There is
little physical action, the primary focus being in the disclosure
of conflicting personalities, but over and above the emotional
pressures generated within the car, external tensions are ever
present. There are bad roads in hostile country, disturbing
encounters with local natives, and constant reminders of the civil
strife that is currently raging in their area.

For a time, it appears that inclement weather may interrupt
their trip, but after stopping overnight at an eccentric old
colonel's resort they make good progress. There are a few minor
accidents; they slide into a ditch once and are run off the road
by a malicious lorry driver, but the high point of the action
occurs when Bobby makes the mistake of confronting a group
of unsupervised native soldiers. One of them seizes the advantage

to release his racial animosities. Bobby is beaten into uncon-
sciousness, but Linda is unmolested, and they manage to reach
safety in the government compound just after nightfall. The
book ends with Bobby finding it impossible to accept the humiliation of his recent experiences. Linda has found out too much
of his private past, and Luke, his black servant, intuitively
judging from Bobby's disheveled appearance, sees too clearly
his vulnerability. "Bobby thought: I will have to leave. But the
compound was safe; the soldiers guarded the gate. Bobby
thought: I will have to sack Luke" (245).

This turn is ironic in light of Bobby's repeated assertions
that "Africa saved my life" and that "my life is here." The
internal drama of the book centers around his growing self-
awareness. In the opening scene, he offers love to a young Zulu
boy, and he often voices an appreciation for natives and scenery,
but as the hours pass on the trip southward, it becomes increasingly apparent that his love for Africa and Africans is illusory.
As he explains to Linda, he has adjusted to his homosexuality,
and he claims to have found his place in life. His delusions
begin to become more apparent, however, with each of his
attempts to communicate with others.

Mutual antagonism marks his relationship with Linda. In their
give-and-take, he confesses the embarrassments of a past mental
breakdown, and under growing pressures he inadvertently displays his ambivalent feelings toward her and all others they
encounter. In spite of his protestations of respect and concern,
he obviously does not comprehend the native mentality. The
vituperative old colonel, maintaining colonial authority on his
premises, has reached a standoff with the natives. His strength
lies in his unmitigated hatred. Unlike him, unfortunately, Bobby
not only misunderstands the local people but he is overly sensitive to their reactions toward him. As a result, he leaves himself
open to the humiliations and abuses that attend his actions.
Thus is he imposed upon by the man at the Hunting Lodge
and by the station attendants at Esher, set upon by the vindictive
soldier at the abandoned schoolhouse, and finally defeated by
the knowing laughter of his own servant.

Both in emotional development and in structural arrangement,
then, the plot of *In a Free State* reflects the same kind of simple,

straightforward method that Naipaul employs in his first five
novels. In keeping with his typical manner, the emphasis is still
on his characters—now, however, not so much showing any
process of development, as disclosing personalities that have
already been formed. He continues to delve into the intricacies
of human relationships, bringing to the surface the frailty, the
foolishness, and the cruelties of mankind. The conciseness of
his expression is tighter in this novella than in any other of his
books. This is both its strength and its weakness. It is unified
and consistent, but so regular in shape that it lacks the passion
and color of Naipaul's best work.

X *The Assembled Structure*

There is no way to determine the ultimate direction Naipaul's
versatile structural technique will take, but for the body of his
extant works it is possible to draw certain tenable conclusions.
In looking back over the eight novels, two separate but related
tendencies appear to emerge from the developing process. The
first three novels pursue the more diverse course. Their casts
are filled with numerous extremely active and colorful characters
who move about and have their being in a strikingly vivid world
wherein chicanery and buffoonery are dominant aspects of life.
The flippant tone and the superficial air of irreverent humor
prompt early designation of these books as farces. Such mistaken understanding led Naipaul in 1958 to respond that he is
writing more seriously and with greater accuracy than most
people know.[10] What makes readers see his work as farce is their
ignorance of the verisimilitude of his fictional representation.
But even with accepting the lifelikeness there is a problem. One
critic observes: "His early books . . . are a series of social comedies.
They are elegant and pithy, with lots of local colour and exotic
appeal."[11] Hitting a more negative note, another reviewer contends that *The Mystic Masseur* is "too clotted with local color."[12]
To this argument Naipaul does not offer rebuttal, but his complaint in "The Regional Barrier," that it is difficult to get an
exotic novel examined on its merits sheds light on his attitude
toward the matter.[13]

    Along with the predominance of local color and provincially

limited characters, another mark of the early fiction is an un-evenness in construction. Naipaul appears to depend too heavily on conventional plot devices at first, and he is not able to sustain a desirable level of esthetic distance. His proximity to the West Indian subject matter keeps him from attaining the objectivity requisite for good art. One result of these primary weaknesses has been the critics' incessant proclivity to pass lightly over the novels and concentrate their attention on the Caribbean society that is being depicted and on the novelist himself. To a certain extent, this explains why criticism—what little of it there is—is often so extraneous to the actual texts, but it does not go far as an excuse for poor criticism.

The second tendency in Naipaul's structural technique begins to define itself for the first time in *Mr Stone and the Knights Companion*. Elements of the change in method are present before this, but the later novels emphasize the developing process, so that in looking back it is possible to detect previous signs of what was to come. (For the moment I am skipping *A House for Mr Biswas*, to return to it in due course. It partakes of the best of both the early and late novels and thus forms a high point, a watershed in the midst of Naipaul's work.) With *Mr Stone and the Knights Companion* Naipaul first succeeds in consistently, and inconspicuously, enclosing the world of his fiction within his own established boundaries. His "framing" technique and his methods of concentrating action around one central figure are greatly improved. He does not carry through with his external frames after *A House for Mr Biswas*, but his predilection for restrictive enclosures continues. The increase in subtlety merely adds to the effectiveness of his method of presentation.

His success in this direction is not achieved, however, without some sacrifice. The strictures on narrative point of view (and the contents of the last four novels are invariably limited to the impressionistically colored worlds of the individual protagonists) severely limit the scope of what is permissible within the hypo-thetical situations that are being treated. John Wain is an articu-late spokesman for the reviewers who object to the method of Naipaul's latter works; of *The Mimic Men*, Wain argues that the restricted narrator is carried too far, that the view is too

slanted, and that secondary characters as a result are flat and
lifeless.[14] Seconding Wain's point and going further, Sara Blackburn feels that *The Mimic Men* is an academic novel, out of
touch with any kind of tangible reality.[15] Yet, the basic tenets
of its structure require a marked degree of abstraction; the plan
of the book calls for the first-person narrator to recount his
autobiography while he is removed from his past action but still
psychologically influenced by it. The primary focal point of this
and the other of the last four novels is the revelation of the
personal attitude. Admittedly, this does not make up for the
loss of breadth, variety, and color that are excluded, but it
explains the necessary conditions which may have led Naipaul
to confine himself as he does.

To clarify the difference between the early and the later
method of construction, it is only necessary to compare *The
Mimic Men* with *The Mystic Masseur*. These works are strikingly
similar in that they are both chronicles which make frequent
use of time shifts to emphasize the evolving attitudes of the
main characters. *The Mystic Masseur* has a variety of characters
who interact, speak in colorful dialect, and undergo various
emotional changes. *The Mimic Men,* on the other hand, discloses
a mental landscape; characters speak, interact, and alter, but
they do so on a limited basis. The comprehensive atmosphere
of the story is constantly dominated by the narrator's reflective
mood. A marked difference between books is underscored in
this sustained mood. The predominant air of the first few novels
is fairly light; in *The Mystic Masseur* a note of cynicism enters
only in the last pages, but by the publication of *Mr Stone and
the Knights Companion* the proportion is reversed; later, in
A Flag on the Island and *In A Free State* there is an inescapable
prevalence of fatalism.

Nothing is to be gained by judging one method to be better,
to the exclusion of the other, for there are advantages as well
as liabilities involved in both. Whereas a measure of variety in
color and perspective is desirable, there is also need for density
and conceptual unity. The darkening tone and increasing seriousness (not that comedy is ever mere play) accompanying Naipaul's
developing structural method have been largely well received by
critics. Karl Miller prefers the complexity of *The Mimic Men;*

it is more pessimistic and no longer leisurely in movement, unlike the "anecdotes of eccentricity and fecklessness" in the first novels.[16] This may be a bit harsh toward Naipaul's early experiments in fiction, but beginning with the fourth book his style, as it increases in complexity, becomes more subtle, consistent, and mature.

A House for Mr Biswas stands in a class to itself, combining the vitality, color, and indomitable spirit of the early novels with the consistency, depth, and maturity of the later ones. The variety available on the one side is mingled with the particularity from the other side. Though *A House for Mr Biswas* is from one point of view representative of a transitional phase in Naipaul's technical development, it is an achievement of classic proportions. There are other factors involved in its power and beauty, but the skeletal structure, the conceptual framework, is a solid foundation on which every other aspect of the novel is firmly based. Moreover, the novels coming after it take strength from the accomplishment of this book.

One of Naipaul's primary weaknesses up to the writing of *A House for Mr Biswas* has been his overly apparent involvement in his material. It is significant that *Mr Stone and the Knights Companion* is a clean break with the West Indian scene. After this novel he returns to the Caribbean subject matter—and he is not actually more serious, just increasingly somber in his treatment—with a darker, but also with a more objective, outlook. The direction he has chosen since this has been inward, into the thought processes of his protagonists. Until he gets to Mr. Biswas his attention seems prone to diffuse itself among colorful but regionally limited characters; thereafter, gathering experiences and sense impressions, he concentrates on figures who in their abstract isolation actually have a more extensive appeal. Mr. Biswas, Mr. Stone, Ralph Singh, Frank, and Bobby embody certain universally recognizable traits. They are in order of appearance more and more withdrawn into themselves, but insight into each of them opens eventually into a broader world.

CHAPTER 3

Character and Setting

I "Local Color"

OF Naipaul's early novels it has been said that others have recorded, but that Naipaul "has given us the very smell, taste and tempo of life in the Indian locations of Trinidad."[1] Nevertheless, his landscapes are not intended and do not appear to be sensuous indulgences in experience simply for the sake of "atmosphere." Settings, perhaps more so in the early than the later books, introduce readers to a significantly new environment only to the extent of providing them with the details necessary to an understanding and acceptance of the exotic situation. The fictional world in which his characters live and breathe is not to be identified with the actual world, but it is (as all fiction is) an outgrowth of the reality depicted.

There is considerable realism and constant attention to minute detail throughout Naipaul's fiction.[2] Even in the humorously light-toned early novels with their surface appearance of farcical improbability, there are serious insights into the basic terms of existence for various levels of island society. Signs of deprivation and desolation pervade almost every place description: panorama and closeup, hill and coast, rural and urban, interior and exterior give the lie to the legendary island paradise. Harbans in an early scene in *The Suffrage of Elvira* is fairly noncommital as he scans the landscape, taking in the nearby jungly hills and valleys, the sugarcane and rice fields, the coastal swamps of Caroni, the oil refinery tanks at Pointe-à-Pierre, the distant suburban houses of San Fernando, and little settlements at the foot of the visible northern mountain range.[3] But his primary interest is not in beauty; he is thinking of the ruts, ravines, and landslides that make the country roads almost impassable, and he likes them that way because the lucrative maintenance contract belongs to him.

Such panoramic views are significantly rare in Naipaul's work, and Harbans' comfortable acceptance of natural hardships (because they are profitable) is highly unusual. In most comparable instances characters are depicted as alienated and frightened. Whenever Mr. Biswas confronts the elements he loses; he is driven by a storm from his incompleted house at Green Vale and suffers a nervous breakdown. Later in the novel he and his entire family are unnerved by their first weekend trip to the seashore; "the noise, the loneliness, the unknown surrounding blackness" (455) force them to huddle together in one room of the large house. Similarly, though on a less vividly descriptive plane Mr. Stone, Ralph Singh, and the leading characters in *A Flag on the Island* and *In a Free State* all come to find that raw nature is not their element. The infrequency of these scenes with extensive views is mute evidence of Naipaul's preference for a smaller, more restrictive canvas.

Focusing in on a typical rural setting, it becomes clear that the harshness in nature is close to the daily lives of all the characters. In its remoteness and desolation, Fuente Grove in *The Mystic Masseur* is like most of the insignificant settlements depicted in the other novels.

Fuente Grove was practically lost. It was so small, so remote, and so wretched, it was marked only on large maps in the office of the Government Surveyor; the Public Works Department treated it with contempt; and no other village even thought of feuding with it. You couldn't really like Fuente Grove. In the dry season the earth baked, cracked, and calcined; and in the rainy season melted into mud. Always it was hot. Trees would have made some difference, but Ganesh's mango tree was the only one. (63)

For this village, as for Elvira in *The Suffrage of Elvira* and rural settlements in *A House for Mr Biswas*, the basis of the invariably depressed economy is agricultural; and the staple crop is sugarcane, for foreign export. Fuente Grove's pathetic attempts at gaiety underscore its squalor. There are few causes to celebrate, but once a year, after harvest, "Fuente Grove made a brave show of gaiety. The half-dozen bullock carts in the village were decorated with pink and yellow and green streamers made from crêpe paper; the bullocks themselves, sad-eyed as ever, wore

bright ribbons in their horns; and men, women and children
rattled the piquets of the carts and beat on pans, singing about
the bounty of God. It was like the gaiety of a starving child" (63-
64). Even to the imagery, degradation prevails, and conditions
in the urban setting offer no relief.

Miguel Street, set in Port of Spain, is a gallery of sketched
failures; prostitution, drinking, and poverty are the rule rather
than the exception where the ambitious few want only to escape
and the hopeless aspire no higher than acquiring reputations
as "characters" or jobs as garbage cart drivers. Mr. Biswas'
mobility brings him into close contact with several areas of
city life. While he is cycling on the outskirts of Pagotes on the
evening of his engagement to Shama, the insubstantiality of the
structures along the road impresses him.

Through unfinished partitions, patched up with box-boards, tin and
canvas, the family clothing could be seen hanging on lengths of
string stretched across the inhabited rooms like bunting; no beds
were to be seen, only a table and chair perhaps, and many boxes.
Twice a day he cycled past these houses, but that evening he saw
them as for the first time. From such failure, which until only that
morning awaited him, he had by one stroke made himself exempt. (83)

In his bid for security, however, it is evident that he is marrying
into an oppressive family. His mother-in-law and Seth rule the
Tulsi dynasty with rigid authority. And the description of the
Tulsi store and house, Hanuman House, resembles nothing more
than a prison. The broad façade of the store belies the cramped,
dark confines within its thick ungainly walls. The courtyard
connecting the store with the living quarters is an enclosed,
damp, and gloomy area. Inside Hanuman House, Mr. Biswas'
eyes pick up the sinister details that complete the picture of
stifling darkness.

Through the doorway at the far end he saw the kitchen. And the
kitchen had mud walls. It was lower than the hall and appeared to
be completely *without light*. The doorway *gaped black; soot stained
the wall* about it and the ceiling just above; so that *blackness seemed
to fill the kitchen* like a solid substance. (78-79, italics mine)

The overall impression of dingy blackness so affects Mr. Biswas that he coins a descriptive epithet "the coal-barrel" for future references to the house.

Emphasis is placed on this particular setting because it exemplifies a significant advance in Naipaul's use of descriptive detail. In *A House for Mr Biswas*, setting definitely becomes an integral aspect of the mental state of his leading character. Scenery has not existed simply for its own sake in earlier works, but with this book the impressions of environment become indispensable to the total literary experience—structure, character, and mood. It should be noted that Naipaul has never played up the peculiarities of Trinidad as exclusively unique; he mentions but does not stress the steel bands and the calypso. His apparent intention has been to establish a concrete environment in which to display his eccentric characters. At times this warrants the "local color" label, but this term is too restrictive to be applied with complete accuracy to his fiction. By the fourth book (*A House for Mr Biswas*), the second phase of Naipaul's development sees the background diminish in value as such, and increase in value as a portion of a mental landscape. The first three novels have disclosed the terms of existence for a complex if depressed way of life.

For the most part, the people are poor and culturally deprived. Professions are out of the reach of all but a few who through bribery, trickery, or less often through success on scholarship tests manage to escape their situation. Most of the families, as is vividly illustrated in *Miguel Street*, are insecurely bound together; the women are slaves to child rearing and household chores; occupations for laborers include seasonal field work, garbage collection, and carpentry. The more fortunate run small shops and enjoy the measured respect of their neighbors. Growing out of their social immobility is their penchant for drawing attention to themselves. Unable to gain recognition through acceptable channels, they assume roles and exaggerate peculiarities so that others notice them. Thus in *Miguel Street* we see Bogart grow into the image of the American film character who bears the same name, Morgan burn his home to the ground in a desperate attempt to gain sympathetic laughter, and "W. C. Tuttle" in *A House for Mr Biswas* irrationally switch from one identity to another—"and heaven knows what pose he would be

in that morning: yogi, weight-lifter, pundit, lorry-driver at
rest" (452).

Such personal eccentricities come together to form a loosely
knit, but a very colorful society. Whatever the ploy at any particular moment, these grotesque bids for recognition are mani-
festations of the Caribbean's special brand of humor. In the
land of Creole-influenced Carnival, where calypso artists and
steel bands compete among themselves for mastery in invective,
witty self-mockery and exaggerated ridicule of individuals and
groups are practically a way of life. Their double-edged humor
transforms the frustrating problems of depressing existence into
laughable absurdity and seems to function as both an avenue of
escape and a defensive mechanism. It allows an acceptable outlet
so that a man can detach himself and make light of his predicament; and in detachment his laughter forms a shield between
him and his unsavory plight. The resultant combination of
fantasy and garish self-indulgence recalls Naipaul's analogous
reference in *The Middle Passage* to the sixteenth-century Spanish picaroon who managed to survive through trickery and by
his wit.

Slavery, the mixed population, the absence of national pride and
the closed colonial system have to a remarkable degree re-created
the attitudes of the Spanish picaroon world. This was an ugly
world, a jungle, where the picaroon hero starved unless he stole,
was beaten almost to death when found out, and had therefore
to get in his blows first whenever possible; where the weak were
humiliated; where the powerful never appeared and were beyond
reach; where no one was allowed any dignity and everyone had to
impose himself. (73)

Aside from the cultural insight afforded here, Naipaul has succeeded in associating the prototype of his fictional world with a
clearly defined literary type. This opens a crucial perspective
into his work. The "Trinidad" and the "Isabella" of the novels
(allowing for exaggeration and the artist's license to be selective) can be understood in terms of what tradition has taught
us to expect of picaresque literature.

A *House for Mr Biswas* in many ways brings together the
central tenets of the picaresque novel that have marked all three

of Naipaul's earlier works. Were Mr. Biswas a more conniving trickster, on the order of a Ganesh or a Baksh, he would fit the prescribed pattern very well. The other elements are all there. We have the chronicle of a lowborn child who because of physical limitations is forced to live by his wits. His story is a series of episodes which though never spectacular are unusual and border often on the absurd. Through his hero's various associations and experiences with people in different places and degrees of life, Naipaul is allowed excellent opportunity to satirize the social classes. With some degree of fantasy in a few episodes the novel is nonetheless predominantly realistic (sometimes scatological) in its attention to vivid detail, its adherence to the plane of low life, and its candid, straightforward presentation. The major factor removing *A House for Mr Biswas* from the category thus defined, and elevating it to a higher level of expression, is its fullness of character development.

II *Internal Landscapes*

Herein, this book signals a turning point, culminating one phase in Naipaul's artistic growth and commencing another. Faithfulness to the depth as well as to the surface color of his creation sets him well on the road to the intensive character studies typical of his later novels. Mr. Biswas is identifiable with the background out of which he attempts desperately, despairingly to escape; he plays the fool, combining realism and fantasy in comic situations which often take on the proportions of melodrama because of his overly emotional involvement with those around him. But at the same time he possesses sensitive, intellectual qualities which, as they are handled by the author, impose his own sense of proportion on the world. In other words, Mr. Biswas, more than the characters before him, utilizes his imagination to come to terms with reality; this is carried to such an extent that it is largely his personal conceptualization rather than perceived objects that occupies the central focus of the novel.

Movement in this direction resolves itself into an interesting pattern in the novels following *A House for Mr Biswas.* In *Mr Stone and the Knights Companion,* the scene where Mr. Stone and his wife are disoriented in the clouds of smoke in the fields near Chysauster illustrates the manner in which inner and outer natures are made to correspond with each other. Fearing the uncertainties of approaching retirement and the accompanying associations with death, Mr. Stone immediately interprets the episode in terms of his predicament. "Mr. Stone never doubted that the incident could be rationally and simply explained. But that hallucinatory moment, when earth and life and senses had been suspended, remained with him. It was like an experience of nothingness, an experience of death" (64). So far, the method echoes that in *A House for Mr Biswas*. In fact, David Ormerod contends that the kind of rootless, helpless suspension experienced by Mr. Stone here and in other episodes represents an overriding leitmotif that pervades all Naipaul's work. "Mr. Stone extends the image until it stands for the basic fact of the entire human state— loneliness and helplessness, set against a sterile landscape."[4]

In *The Mimic Men* further development of the pattern may be seen in Ralph Singh's determination (expressed intermittently throughout his story) to establish order and coherence in his life by writing it up as history, "clearing the decks" as he expresses it, and setting parentheses about segments that do not comply with his specifications. Then in *A Flag on the Island* the effects of imposing personal concepts on reality are carried to their ironic conclusion. As Henry warns Frank,

> Frankie, I think you trying too hard with Mano. You should watch it. You see what happen to Mrs Lambert. You know, I don't think people want to do what they say they want to do. I think we always make a lot of trouble for people by helping them to get what they say they want to get. (194)

Henry is right; Frank's interference not only results in Mano's suicide, Henry's unhappy domestication, the destruction of Mr. Lambert's house, and general corruption of island values, but also in his own spiritual degradation. In the island's transformation from unspoiled indolence to industrious frenzy may be seen a parallel to the narrator's internal mood; ironically, what he has helped to bring about escapes his control. From emotional identification with external reality, then, to the arbitrary imposition of personal concepts on it, the pattern follows its course.

No release is offered in *In a Free State*. At various times, Bobby and Linda view themselves as participants in a film; the landscape reminds them of Bergman or of a John Ford western.[5] The artificiality of their existence and their sterility are underscored by the absence of effective communication. Their protective roles separate them not only from each other but also from the outer world in which they are attempting to live.

An immediate result of this developing process of introversion is the noticeable shift away from the prominence of local color and by degrees a discernible movement toward abstraction and less particularly identifiable localities. Dialect, for instance, diminishes in importance as the West Indianness of the fiction is deemphasized. In this respect, however, Naipaul's treatment of language has not undergone as much of a change as might be expected. There has been little reason for alteration because in the scenes in early books where carefully selective dialect occurs it has been standardized so that much of the strangeness is eliminated at the outset. The main features of the native language he preserves are the simplified grammar, limited vocabulary (very few completely foreign words of African and Indian origin), and slightly unique but plain syntactical structures, with normal spelling. Though this may do a slight injustice in some of the early novels to the spoken Creole of the island, it has the advantage of being readily comprehensible to the metropolitan English reader, and it retains enough of the authentic flavor to convey the lyrical rhythm and effervescent spirit of the vernacular. Moreover, his normalized version is not far removed from what the increasingly educated lower and middle classes speak—a language Kenneth Ramchand names "West Indian Standard English."[6] A humorous episode in *The Mystic Masseur* illustrates the predicament of islanders who are caught between their indigenous and their formally acquired language. Ganesh, inspired by the desire to publish, instigates a campaign to elevate domestic conversation.

> One day he said, "Leela, is high time we realise that we living in a British country and I think we shouldn't be shame to talk the people language good."
> Leela was squatting at the kitchen *chulha,* coaxing a fire from

dry mango twigs. Her eyes were red and watery from the smoke.
"All right, man."
    "We starting now self, girl."
    "As you say, man."
    "Good. Let me see now. Ah, yes. Leela, have you lighted the fire?
No, just gimme a chance. Is 'lighted' or 'lit,' girl?"
    "Look, ease me up, man. The smoke going in my eye."
    "You ain't paying attention girl. You mean the smoke *is* going in
your eye."
    Leela coughed in the smoke. "Look, man. I have a lot more to do
than sit scratching, you hear. Go talk to Beharry." (71-72)

The talk with Beharry is equally unsatisfactory, and Ganesh
gives up the attempt.

Naipaul's skill remains remarkably high as he smoothly alter-
nates between levels of the language used by characters and
the standard English of the ostensible author, whether the setting is West Indian, strictly the purest British, or, as with
portions of the last three novels, a landscape predominantly of
the mind. The steady restriction and normalization of dialect,
then, help the smooth transition after *A House for Mr Biswas*
into a more abstract atmosphere where the mental and emotional
perception of the character takes precedence over outward
manifestation of regional differences.

The change is one of emphasis. What happens is that episodes which might at first have been categorized as simply local
color because of their superficial regional limitations or farcical
because of their extravagance are toned down and handled more
seriously. The trend is slightly noticeable in *A House for Mr
Biswas* and marked in subsequent works in keeping with a matur-
ing, increasingly complex style of writing. Following the pattern
I have described above, elements of background and setting not
only become significant because of the part they play in character revelation; they evolve into images and motifs which unify
and integrate all phases of textual development. In an obvious
sense, for example, the house in *A House for Mr Biswas* gains
its symbolic eminence because of the background of deprivation,
crowding, and insecurity which makes the possession of a private
dwelling such an ideal goal for an islander. The various lodging
places, each with its individual drawbacks—Hanuman House,

authoritarian and oppressive in its communalism; the houses at
The Chase and Green Vale, unbearable burdens because of the
uncertainties surrounding their construction; the Short Hills
and Port of Spain buildings, dispiriting because of their rapid
deterioration under the hands of the exploitative Tulsi family—
form a backdrop and simultaneously motivate Mr. Biswas
toward his goal. The impact of setting is nowhere more explicit
than in Mr. Biswas' memory of the trees and the Tulsi-owned
barracks where he lived at Green Vale.

Half the leaves were dead; the others, at the top, were a *dead green.*
It was as if all the trees had, at the same moment, been *blighted in
luxuriance,* and *death* was spreading at the. same pace from all the
roots. But *death* was forever held in check. The tonguelike leaves
of *dead* green turned slowly to the brightest yellow, became brown
and thin as if scorched, curled downwards over the other *dead* leaves
and did not fall. And new leaves came, as sharp as daggers; but there
was *no freshness* to them; they came into the world *old, without
a shine,* and *only grew longer before they too died....*
As soon as he saw the barracks Mr Biswas decided that the time
had come for him to build his own house, by whatever means. (185,
italics mine)

It is the way things appear to him that drives him forward.
    Environment plays a similar role in *Mr Stone and the Knights
Companion.* The drabness of the circle of friends in which Mr.
Stone moves reflects his own petty realm of existence. Outside
his window the seasons are marked by a tree with which he
identifies; and his mental state colors its meaning as his hopes and
anxieties fluctuate. "The contemplation of this living object re-
assured him of the solidity of things. He had grown to regard
it as part of his own life, a marker of his past, for it moved
through time with him. The new leaves of spring, the hard green
of summer, the naked black branches of winter, none of these
things spoke of the running out of his life. They were only a
reminder of the even flowing of time, of his mounting experience, his lengthening past" (20). Serenity imaged forth in the
tree here is balanced later by the fear elicited by the blinding
smoke. It is significant, too, that the smoke contributes to his

urge for order and stability just as the frightening trees had
moved Mr. Biswas.

There are too many such examples of the affinity between
mental state and setting in *The Mimic Men* to detail them all,
but they include innumerable references to Ralph Singh's deeply
rooted preferences for mountains and snow as opposed to his
native elements, sand and sea. Out of his island environment
he is also (appropriately) obsessed by images of ships and
shipwrecks; and closely associated with his experiences in
England is his sensitivity to the shades of light. "They talk of
the light of the tropics and Southern Spain. But there is no light
like that of the temperate zone. It was a light that gave solidity
to everything and drew colour out from the heart of objects. To
me, from the tropics, where night succeeded day abruptly, dusk
was new and enchanting" (22). Repeated references to these and
other aspects of environment and background recur with such
frequency in phrases and scenes that they constitute thematic
motifs which weave in and out of the narrative, linking and
drawing together the scattered moods and ideas of the speaker.

The same technique appears in *A Flag on the Island* where
local culture, folk dances and music, and native literature have
been corrupted through exposure to foreign influences. Frank,
the narrator, has avoided returning to the island, and when he is
forced by Hurricane Irene to land there, his fear begins to
deepen immediately. Local color comes to the fore in several
passages, but even when it is most obvious, the narrator's mood
dominates. As in the previous novels, details accumulate according to the dictates of his feelings. The flag now waving over
the island appears (as do the names and labels which mean a
great deal to Frank) as the symbolic recognition of its existence. Before the flag, before the islanders had gained attention
in the world's eyes, they had felt unreal. Now, even though they
all play roles and have assumed a false identity to satisfy the
tourist market, they at least feel that they exist.

Frank, apparently suffering guilt from his contribution to the
island's spiritual sickness, recalls his past visit—the carnival,
steel bands, and the calypso—and he wants to escape to a jungle
clearing, to become an ascetic recluse. There is no way of
escape, though, as Selma tells him: "there are no more islands."

He is stranded, as is Bobby in *In a Free State*. Frank can always sail away from the island again, but he really has no place to go. Bobby cannot leave the safety of the government compound; he can, however, dismiss the servant who has invaded his private sphere and by this gesture attempt to regain his precious isolation. The movement for both of these men, then, is inward, away from that with which they can no longer cope.

Emphasis on mental states in these last novels has not been in lieu of reality. In fact, a mood or a feeling is just as much a part of reality as the most durable adamant. Whatever the setting—the English middle-class drawing room, a metropolitan hotel, or the emerging Caribbean or African nation—Naipaul continually employs his sharp eye for telling detail and expressive gesture. The difference from earlier accuracy is in his not relying upon localized details. He selects those that are recognizable for their human rather than for their regional association. With the abatement of his earlier comic spirit he has turned more and more to the common elements in humanity for serious analysis and exposition. He is writing what Oscar R. Dathorne describes as "a new kind of realism in which . . . the writers are more concerned with human situations in a setting that is every West Indian island and yet none at all."[7] Actually, the technique is not very new; it appears at least as far back in American literature as the works of Stephen Crane and is simply a form of "impressionism."

This is not to imply that Naipaul is an impressionist, but merely that he resorts to the method when it suits his purpose. That he prefers an imaginative interpretation of reality to a simple photographic reproduction is brought out definitely in a statement he made in 1967. "The artist who, for political or humanitarian reasons, seeks only to record abandons half his responsibility. . . . He does not impose a vision on the world."[8] As Naipaul makes clear with increasing assurance in successive novels beginning with *A House for Mr Biswas*, background and surroundings influence the shaping of character, and character, in turn, gives human color and meaning to the total environment. It should come as no surprise to find in *A Flag on the Island* the protagonist voicing the opinion that "all landscapes are in the end only in the imagination" (149).

III *Character and Setting*

Such a philosophical statement reveals a figure with a degree of self-awareness that is far removed from the comparatively naïve and shallow eccentrics portrayed in the earlier books. As Naipaul has grown in experience and his style has become more serious, his works have revealed a depth that was at first barely visible beneath a surface distractingly patched with local color.

These characters are only credible in the setting of Trinidad, of which they are true products. . . . They all seem to lead a haphazard existence, without well-understood principles, without efficient organization of any kind. They are as unorthodox in matters of religion as in politics, borrowing from each creed only what suits them. They are sometimes dishonest, though they do not resent it when they are found out, and they are mostly unreliable. Yet, underneath it all, one feels their humaneness, their genuine generosity, and, in spite of some prejudices and occasional squabbles, their tolerance even in matters of race.[9]

Before the achievement of the classical Mohun Biswas and the meticulously executed psychological studies of the mature novels, Naipaul's characters are often delightfully lively and vividly dramatized, but they lend themselves too readily to the sort of typecasting that obscures individuality. On the surface, Ganesh, Ramlogan, and Baksh all closely resemble wily, picaresque tricksters; others are identifiable largely by personal idiosyncrasies which function as a shorthand method of character portrayal. Enjoyable as they are, most of the secondary figures end almost as they are when they are introduced, showing little or no real development during the story. What exposition of character there is, however, is executed with great skill, either through economical disclosures by the narrator or through the yet more artistically satisfying revelations brought about by dramatically expressive gestures, dialogues, and interactions.

Naipaul's skill at touching the minute detail to exact the maximum desired effect is evidenced repeatedly in *The Mystic Masseur*. Beharry the teetotaling barkeeper never drank "because he was a good Hindu and because, as he told Ganesh, 'It have nothing like a clear head, man.' Also, his wife didn't approve" (64). The real order of priorities here is unmistakable. His being henpecked is never made an issue, but through subtle indicators it becomes nonetheless obvious. He never repeats his wife's name, referring to her always as his son's mother, "Suruj Mooma,"[10] and he allows her tongue free rein to criticize him and his actions. When he speaks he becomes like a mouse, working (as is often pointed out in the text) "his small mouth nervously up and down as though he were nibbling" (65). Probably as a learned reflex he seldom asserts himself, but in his unashamed subservience to the greatness he recognizes in Ganesh he becomes a valuable ally—a scaled-down Panza to the Masseur's Quixote.

Other secondary characters who play off each other very well are also important in shaping the protagonist's course. Ramlogan always looks out for his own best interests, but when he thinks he can get his second daughter married off cheaply he makes the costly mistake of underestimating his son-in-law's cunning. At the kedgeree-eating ceremony the impassive bridegroom humiliates him into raising a considerable dowry. The old rogue's discomfiture in this comic scene temporarily establishes Ganesh as a hero in the eyes of the villagers, but more importantly it initiates the feud that persists in fluctuating intensity until near the end of the story.

Inheriting much of her father's avarice, Leela acts as both a spur and a tool for her husband. Her innocent loyalty to Ramlogan is an asset to Ganesh at first because the tale she carries back to her father frightens him so that he is desirous of making peace. Normalcy settles over the marriage, with petty squabbles and ritual wife-beatings, but Leela is dissatisfied with their meager existence. As her curt response to her husband's explanation for his unprofitable inactivity indicates, she possesses a deftly cutting tongue.

> "Leela, is the thing everybody who want to write have to face. Poverty and sickness is what every writer have to suffer."
> "But you ain't writing man."
> Ganesh didn't reply. (83)

This exchange ends in her running away, but it leads to positive results. In order to regain her, Ganesh diligently writes and publishes the first of his many books. Other conflicts with Leela, however, almost bring on real trouble. Later, as jealousy of her

more successful sister and material desires gain in strength, she
resorts to darker machinations. She instigates a scheme whereby
she and Ramlogan monopolize the taxi service that transports
clients to the mystic in Fuente Grove. Hard feelings develop,
but in the power struggle that ensues Ganesh triumphs; and
again he turns Leela's subterfuge to advantage, utilizing the
additional income to lay the foundations for his future political
career.

Leela's development, limited as it is, is about as extensive
as that of any other woman in Naipaul's fiction, and it is significant that among the females depicted in *The Mystic Masseur*
there are prominent similarities. "The Great Belcher" stands
alone in her timely visits to advise Ganesh as to the best moves
at crucial points in his career, but aside from her sagacity and
the wind (to which she attributes her interminable belching)
and her attested reliance on the dependability of "King George"
(who deserts her) there is little else to her personality. Resem-
blances among the other females are especially pronounced in
that there is a chain of mimicry linking them to each other.
Just as the women preparing for Ganesh's wedding adopt belching and complaining of the wind, after The Great Belcher, so
with Soomintra, Leela's well-to-do city sister, a series of affectations originates. With new wealth, Leela assumes her sister's
grievances over housing, fatigue, and the desperate need for
a vacation. Then in turn, Suruj Mooma is afflicted with the same
maladies.

Naipaul employs a rather simple device to eliminate the
possibility of his lightly sketched figures losing their personal
individualities. For each of the minor and even most of the
major characters he designates a peculiarity and by reiterating
this "tag" in connection with the person at intervals throughout
the story he effectively avoids confusion. This singling out of
prominent features and dwelling almost exclusively on them
closely resemble the method of caricature, but a better explanation of the technique is to be found, again, in local color. As any
observer of Caribbean life can verify, native society abounds in
eccentrics who flaunt their idiosyncrasies. Deriving from these
cultivated quirks are nicknames often having the ring of epithet.
Thus in *The Mystic Masseur* "The Great Belcher" and "King

George" may be accounted for. Others, without actually acquiring the name, also display similarly indicative "tags": Ramlogan defends "cha'acter and sensa values" and "radicals" in the family; Beharry nibbles like a mouse; Soomintra is tired and needs a vacation; Suruj Mooma expounds upon the disadvantages of education. There is even "the boy" participating actively in Ganesh's campaign who, probably because of his immaturity and enthusiasm, remains just "the boy." Likewise in *The Suffrage of Elvira* there are the shadowy Miss Short and Miss Tall, and in *A Flag on the Island* there are three stock figures named Chippy, Bippy, and Tippy.

These concise little classifications are not likely to be always reliably accurate, but they facilitate quick insights into the types of people being treated and allow the quickly flowing narrative to progress uninterruptedly. The method of abbreviating characters serves especially well in the first four books which, taken together, offer an extensive collection of briefly sketched but delightfully intriguing individuals.

Similarities between *The Mystic Masseur* and *The Suffrage of Elvira* are so close that figures could be (two actually are) transposed from one to the other. Even though Harbans would seem to be the logical protagonist, being the prime candidate for election, he is actually almost incidental to the main action. More acted upon than acting, he is constantly moaning and looking absently at the backs of his hands while the narrator conveys his thoughts. His place is usurped by a conniving rogue whose resemblance to Ramlogan and Ganesh (the two retained from the first novel) demands comparison. Like Ramlogan, Mazurus Baksh is a family man, proprietor of a small shop, full of talk, and willing to use any trick to gain personal advantage.

It is no ordinary conspirator who after selling his allegiance to Harbans can finagle two further bribes, enter his own candidacy, and run a profitably unsuccessful campaign before swinging his bloc of votes in the direction for which he was originally paid. He differs from Ramlogan in that he is slightly less melodramatic; and his higher degree of self-awareness allows him more flexibility. Whereas Ramlogan rants and cries when he is bested by Ganesh in *The Mystic Masseur* or by Chittaranjan in *The Suffrage of Elvira,* Baksh, when he is not drunk, will resort to cool calculation or assume the clown, depending upon which will serve him best in the given situation. In response to a racial slur from Chittaranjan, Baksh proceeds to turn injury into advantage. "You say it yourself. Negro and Muslim is one. All right. Preacher getting every Muslim vote in Elvira" (129). But when he realizes at the end of the race that his hand is played out, even then he rises above defeat in laughter. Though he is one of the official candidates, he manages to hire himself to the government as a public announcer, and as the election returns come in he entertains the crowd with a joke on himself.

"Another result. From Cordoba, station number one. Another result. From Cordoba One. Final result. Baksh nought. Baksh nought."
The crowd appreciated the joke. (220)

If Baksh were to be compared with Ganesh, he would be found to be a less fully developed character, but his sense of humor preserves him from the frigid cynicism that ultimately overwhelms the famous mystic. From the fledgling teacher who fails because he "informs rather than forms," to the conscientious massager who refuses to gull people he cannot heal, to the dynamic leader who actually represents his constituency, we see the good side of Ganesh. From his steadily increasing assurance as he handles Ramlogan, Leela, and his political opponents we come to realize his carefully restrained power to act decisively. But even though it is only latent at the beginning, in retrospect we can also observe the weakness that undermines his rather idealistic nature. He is insecure in his identity (as a boy he allows friends to call him Gareth rather than his Indian name), and he is not without ambition (he makes big promises and insists that the printer save the type face for his first edition so that he can fulfill the later demands for copies). Ambition and insecurity cause no problems, however, even after the humiliation of the meal at the governor's house, until he allows his reach to exceed his grasp. Then disillusionment overtakes him. The breaking point is his failure to cope with the cane workers' strike and his subsequent discovery that the entire fiasco was rigged to enrich some of the very people he was attempting to help. From this point on, abandoning both his role as champion of the people and his Indian name, he accepts political corruption and the emoluments that accrue to those who "play the game."

This is the Ganesh whose name is referred to in *The Suffrage of Elvira* and who makes a brief appearance in *Miguel Street*. In the final analysis, he is not really an admirable figure, but everyone respects him because he has won eminence. The fact that he is in a position to receive bribes, that he is above the law and the vicissitudes of existence on Miguel Street puts him in the realm of the ideal. In a sense, it is fitting that he, the first of Naipaul's many lively characters, should descend as a jaded *deus ex machina* to rescue the young narrator of the third novel—the book that serves well as a veritable living picture album of the kinds of individuals who populate the world of the early fiction. "*Miguel Street* is a funny book; eccentricity, failure, inefficiency, or immaturity are gently mocked and shaped into comedy. Dialogue is the author's main instrument for building up his characters. The invective and racy dialect he uses and his choice of suggestive incidents produce funny and disarming personages."[11]

Techniques of characterization utilized in this work are the same as those previously discussed; the major new element, perhaps, is added emphasis on an obvious human sympathy. The narrator, who is young and immature for the most part, displays a heartfelt concern for the plight of others by withholding his laughter from that of the crowd when he realizes how deeply someone can be hurt. "Big Foot's" cowardice and Laura's incomprehensible love for her eight illegitimate children are to be exempted from the ridicule of the street. Apparently an unspoken code of propriety leads Hat to punish Boyee for his insensitivity in questioning Laura's despair over her daughter's following in her footsteps. Adding greatly to the story, Hat's point of view complements the narrator's ingenuousness; he is more thoughtful than most of his friends, a kind of homespun philosopher whose wisdom fails him in the end. His wry glosses on street incidents bring to the surface the deeper human qualities that underlie all of Naipaul's creations. And the fact that he too falls victim to human frailty makes him all the more meaningful as a character.

The appearance of Ganesh in *Miguel Street* is a fitting climax in the early stage of Naipaul's development. The pundit's being presented as already having attained fame is also a major reason for handling *Miguel Street* as third, in the order of its publication, rather than first, in the order of its writing. But in the final analysis, the simplistically overt chronological ordering of events and the overlapping use of characters—Ramlogan, and Ganesh, and Man-Man, and even Chittaranjan's brother who is mentioned in *The Suffrage of Elvira* and then is Hat's lawyer in *Miguel Street*—smack of cuteness and may be detrimental to the integrity of the individual novels. The practice invites the reader to look from one book to the other and thus threatens the internal unity of each self-contained creation. Logically, this show of virtuosity may be excused by the light tone and easygoing style of the works themselves, but Naipaul is a serious artist, and with *Miguel Street* he seems to have realized that by playing so loosely over the surface of his structure he is endangering the inner depths of his fiction. It still remains for him to utilize his talents in proportioning a well-rounded, fully developed novel. And this requirement is admirably met in the story of Mohun Biswas.

IV   *The "Absurd Man"*

It is a mark of the brilliance in the creation of Mr. Biswas that he defies simple classification. Quite understandably, too, this character has drawn easily more critical attention than any other of Naipaul's protagonists. The designation "hero" is avoided at this point because in the minds of some critics there are reservations about his heroic proportions.[12] It is true that none of Mr. Biswas' individual acts is of much significance by itself. He is an unimportant man who in many ways is even petty, but the complete story of his life turns out to be greater than the sum of its mundane parts. In fact, Gordon Rohlehr detects universal implications in the terms of his highly personal struggle.

Biswas is Everyman, wavering between identity and nonentity, and claiming his acquaintance with the rest of men.... If Biswas represents all the things I feel he does, it is because he is fully presented as a person whose every quirk and idiosyncrasy we know, in a world whose every sight, sound and smell is recorded with fidelity and precision. Whatever is suggested of the numinous and universal, is conveyed through a fidelity to the concrete and particular. Landscape and life are not treated as isolated, but both conform to the artist's unity of purpose.[13]

According to this estimate, it appears that the realism that is sometimes attributable to "local color" in earlier works has become in the fourth book a necessary "fidelity to the concrete and particular." Authentic features of the West Indian scene are conscientiously preserved—dialect, customs, natural setting—but the individuals depicted are first of all human beings and in spite of obvious superficial differences are like middle- and lower-class people the world over. They have the same problems, feel the same driving needs, and suffer the same frustrations.

Mr. Biswas may be an archetypal "Everyman" but if so he is a modernized version, for in his confrontation with the vicissitudes of life he expresses an acute awareness of the absurd. In each direction he turns he finds obstacles to his happiness, and he can discover no reasons for his predicament. Thus he conforms to Camus' fundamental definition of the "absurd" which is neither a quality of the world, nor simply an idea born in man, but a result of their being situated together. The absurd man "feels within him his longing for happiness and for reason. The absurd is born of this confrontation between the human need and the unreasonable silence of the world."[14] After the novels of the 1950's and 1960's, this type of literary figure is not new; it has been made familiar by the likes of Salinger, Bellow, and Malamud. Biswas partakes of this class and he also owes a great deal to the nineteenth-century school of social realists, whose leading characters, like Dickens' and Hardy's, exemplify the contemporary society out of which they grow as they attempt to redeem it. Biswas, then, simultaneously embodies the alienated modern man and the sensitive though ineffectual reformer. His desperate bid for improvement is a self-centered one, but as Rohlehr points out, "The purity of motive and truth to instinct and necessity which marked Biswas's struggle against an apparently indestructible system make his rebellion an affirmation of universal values; transform it from being a sordid personal struggle to one undertaken on behalf of the group."[15]

Rohlehr's article emphasizes the rebelliousness of Biswas' nature; yet he does not begin as a rebel; the role slowly grows upon him and is never his dominant attribute. First of all, he is merely sensitively aware of the grossness and the beauty that surround him. Out of this awareness grows a romantic dissatisfaction with his limitations. His reading of Samuel Smiles suggests a remedy. "Mr Biswas saw himself in many Samuel Smiles heroes: he was young, he was poor, and he fancied he was struggling. But there always came a point when resemblance ceased. The heroes had rigid ambitions and lived in countries where ambitions could be pursued and had a meaning. He had no ambition, and in this hot land, apart from opening a shop or buying a motorbus, what could he do?" (71). With no avenue immediately open to success he simply waits. Still the romantic, he expects love and beauty to descend from above and reveal the efficacy of his faith. While in this lethargic state he suddenly discovers what he believes will exempt him from failure—the imposing Tulsis' house, marriage, and security. Throughout the novel houses stand for stability, refuge from the shapeless outer world, but Hanuman House, as its façade suggests, is too well organized. "Hanuman House stood like an alien white fortress. The concrete walls looked as thick as they were, and when the narrow doors of the Tulsi Store on the ground floor were closed the House became bulky, impregnable and blank. The side walls were windowless, and on the upper two floors the windows were mere slits in the façade" (73). As he discovers, he has simply exchanged one problem for another. He has imprisoned himself; he is trapped, and the only recourse that occurs to him is flight.

Though his running from the burden he has unpremeditatedly assumed in marriage is described by Naipaul in terms of rebellion, his reaction, at least at first, is more one of evasion. Romantic dissatisfaction evolves into a desperate need to escape. Like Ganesh and Teacher Francis previously, Biswas turns out to be what Ramlogan would call a "radical"; he will not accommodate himself to the pattern. Unlike his predecessors in the role, however, he has too much feeling, too much ambivalent empathy with what antagonizes him simply to begin attempting to change things. His natural reaction to stress is to escape; when he fears insecurity he runs to the rigidly structured Tulsis' house; when he feels his individual identity threatened by the communal pressures there, he returns to the uncertainties of the disorganized world outside. It is not that he is indecisive; he just equivocates because he cannot find a satisfactory middle ground between extremes. Thus it is that in spite of what he knows will happen he tries repeatedly, in Seth's words, to "paddle his own canoe." "Biswas the paddler" moves in the common stream, but he cannot stifle the urge to resist the current.

Throughout the book, Biswas' escapist tendencies manifest themselves in a variety of forms. At The Chase he paints blissful scenes: "He painted cool, ordered forest scenes, with gracefully curving grass, cultivated trees ringed with friendly serpents, and floors bright with perfect flowers; not the rotting, mosquito-infested jungle he could find within an hour's walk" (164). At different times he turns to reading—to edifying self-improvement guides, to philosophy, but most often to satisfy his insatiable yearning for the outside world "he read novels that took him there" (186). From his reading he is inspired to write, and his creative efforts take two distinct forms. "Whatever his mood and however painful his subject, he became irreverent and facetious as soon as he began to write" (165). This first style stands him in good stead when he becomes a reporter for Mr. Burnett's newspaper: "For the facetiousness that came to him as soon as he put pen to paper, and the fantasy he had hitherto dissipated in quarrels with Shama and in invective against the Tulsis, were just the things Mr Burnett wanted" (291-92). His second style takes the form of the unfinished "escape stories." These are inevitably directed against the oppressive surroundings that threaten to defeat him. "The hero, trapped into marriage, burdened with a family, his youth gone, meets a young girl. She is slim, almost thin, and dressed in white. She is fresh, tender, unkissed; and she is unable to bear children. Beyond the meeting the stories never went" (311).

At least these kinds of escape lead toward something positive; others are purely negative. At Green Vale he becomes a recluse, locking himself in his room and refusing to let Shama touch him. This segment of his life is crucial to his development because it takes him into the depths of despair. He suffers a complete nervous breakdown and he ends up making one of his

more humiliating returns to Hanuman House because of it; but
from this point on he realizes that "the second to second agony
and despair of those days at Green Vale had given him an
experience of unhappiness against which everything had now
to be measured" (273). His return from this "dark night of the
soul" is accomplished through surrender. By the act of just giving
up, his fears abate, and he finds respite in the dark, silent void
of the comforting stability of Hanuman House.

After Green Vale, all of the evasive reactions, heretofore signs
of his inadequacy and weakness, undergo a marked change. He
continues to rage and throw impotent temper tantrums, but
upon his recovery at Hanuman House he has gained invaluable
confidence in the resilience of his spirit. "He was going out into
the world, to test it for its power to frighten. The past was coun-
terfeit, a series of cheating accidents. Real life, and its especial
sweetness, awaited; he was still beginning" (274-75). Of course
it takes little time for the world to revive his fears, but the
boundless faith disclosed in these thoughts never deserts him for
long.

His animosity toward the Tulsis remains alive, but since their
outmoded authoritarian structure soon begins to disintegrate
from within, there is little need for him to instigate active rebellion. An excellent register of Mr. Biswas' progress may be
seen in the decline of the Tulsis that coincides with his own rise
in fortune. Hanuman House itself and especially Seth and Mrs.
Tulsi fairly well embody the incomprehensible forces that
threaten his well-being. Were it not for the fact that Biswas'
own inner drives are his greatest adversaries, Mrs. Tulsi would
best qualify for the role of antagonist. As it is, when her authority
begins to fail, the prospects for his growth are improved.

His attempt to build a house at Short Hills results in failure,
but he is definitely gaining independence through his journalism. His path, however, remains a rough one; he still reveals
some of his most unattractive traits. Looking back over his dismal
career he begins to complain of what might have been, and as
is quite human he weakly shoves blame off on his father, his
mother, the Tulsis, his wife, and more and more on the *Sentinel*.
An immediate reason for the emphasis on his employer may be
found in the nature of his Deserving Destitutes assignment.

"The *Sentinel* could not have chosen a better way of terrifying Mr Biswas, of reviving his dread of the sack, illness or sudden disaster. Day after day he visited the mutilated, the defeated, the futile, and the insane living in conditions not far removed from his own: in suffocating rotting wooden kennels, in sheds of boxboard, canvas and tin, in dark and sweating concrete caverns" (398). The effects of such conditions on any man would be sickening; on Biswas they are almost devastating.

Combined with the Tulsis at home, the pressures at the office, and the degradation of the slums where he has to work, his world becomes increasingly somber in tone. He finally manages to move into his own house, that constant symbolic goal of his quest for meaningful independence; but the meaning drains out of his existence. "He grew dull and querulous and ugly. Living had always been a preparation, a waiting. And so the years had passed; and now there was nothing to wait for" (528). At last, his other romantic ideals having proved inadequate, he turns his attention to his children; and again his faith is revived. He dies knowing that his son is ungrateful, but his daughter and Shama prove to be a source of pleasure to him to the end. It is finally in the little things that he learns to find happiness, in the things closest to him, his plants, his sadly insecure house, and the people he has grown to love.

The conclusion of Biswas' life, like the rest of it, is unspectacular. His view of the world as it is reflected in the way he lived is faulty and shortsighted; but as Rohlehr shows, his struggle is not without its touches of heroism. "Indeed Biswas is at times petty, cowardly, and contemptible, and part of the book's triumph is that Naipaul has been able to present a hero in all his littleness, and still preserve a sense of the man's inner dignity."[16] His romantic, self-centered egotism has denied him until it is almost too late the simple pleasure of sympathetic human companionship and understanding, but then he is the one who has had to pay the price of loneliness, the kind of loneliness, in fact, that lies at the heart of the human condition. Perhaps his single most saving attribute, that which compensates for all that is contemptible in him, is the unfailing presence—always underlying his futile efforts to escape—of his faith in the value of the attempt. This is what keeps him going; this is what makes

him appear a rebel. He refuses to conform, to give up his identity, to allow sordid existence to grind him under. I should not
go so far as David Ormerod to compare Biswas' death with that
of King Lear, but his courageous struggle in the face of absurdity
and the quality of faith it reveals is truly admirable.[17]

Aside from the fuller development of individuals, characterization techniques in this novel are remarkably similar to those
employed in the earlier books. Mute evidence of Biswas' tower-
ing ego is in the fact that he overshadows most of the minor
figures. He is so caught up in himself most of the time that he
is brought up sharply from time to time with the discovery that
Shama, whom he has taken to be bland and unthinking, has
contacts with the outer world and ideas and opinions of her
own. Through Biswas' habit of forming comic epithets to cate-
gorize others, Naipaul succeeds in quite naturally repeating the
"tags" and distinguishing characteristics of the people who crowd
into Hanuman House. An especially effective use of the device
occurs in its application to faceless groups such as "the children,"
"the widows," and "the readers and learners." By lumping them
together this way he subtly underscores their lack of individuality
and deftly suggests the impression they have made on the protagonist. This of course has a direct influence on the reader's
response to Biswas' world. "Since Naipaul's art relies heavily
on repetition or allusion to something already established, each
episode consolidates our first impression of the crowded, noisy,
ritualized life and single-attribute people."[18] In his refinement
of this technique, Naipaul points the way to his method in the
later novels wherein to a greater extent than in A House for Mr
Biswas practically all phases of characterization and setting are
subsumed under the personality of the central characters.

There are several differences between A House for Mr Biswas
and the next novel, Mr Stone and the Knights Companion. The
shift in setting from a Caribbean island to the London suburbs
is but one. There is also a drastic reduction in the amount of
time covered in each book, from spanning parts of three genera-
tions of a West Indian family to just the last two years before
an aging Englishman's retirement. Another marked change appears in the darkening tone as action and drama give way in

Mr. Stone's rather drab and constricted life to reflection and faltering gestures.

V   *"The Little Man"*

In effect Mr. Stone appears to be a Prufrockian "little man." He is a sadly comic figure living in a nondescript, middle-class suburban world which he likes to think of as well ordered and stable in its unhurried movement.

Life was something to be moved through. Experiences were not to be enjoyed at the actual moment; pleasure in them came only when they had been, as it were, docketed and put away in the file of the past, when they had become part of his 'life', his 'experience', his career. It was only then that they acquired colour, just as colour came truly to Nature only in a coloured snapshot or a painting, which annihilated colourless, distorting space. (18-19)

The contrast with Biswas' harried conception of reality is remarkable; just as remarkable too are the similarities between this and Ralph Singh's view of the order that he creates for himself as he records the acts of his life.

But late in life, at the age of sixty-two, less than three years before retirement Mr. Stone's order begins to break down. The vague uneasiness that has been growing in him for some time suddenly comes into focus upon his chance reading of an advertisement. The phrase "those who doubt the coming of Spring" jumps out at him. With approaching retirement, idleness, loneliness, old age, and after that the empty void of death staring him in the face, he discovers that he has very good reason to doubt the coming of spring.

It is while he is still recovering from this shocking revelation that he makes an acquaintance which largely reshapes his quiet routine. At a party given by his friends the Tomlinsons, he meets widow Springer (if there is symbolism in her name, surely it is ironic). After a brief courtship he marries her, and the order he has only recently begun to question is abruptly altered. As is reflected in his changing conception of the aspects of familiar surroundings, the former referents upon which he has depended to confirm his security are no longer helpful. The serenity of his favorite tree becomes a reproach; his neighbors the "Monster" and the "Male," as he designates them, seem only to be going through useless motions; his own empty gestures have become fraudulent posturings for his wife and Miss Millington whose helpful solicitations for their "man" only add to his feelings of emptiness. "And he had a realization, too upsetting to be more than momentarily examined, that all that was solid and immutable and enduring about the world, all to which man linked himself (the Monster watering her spring flowers, the Male expanding his nest), flattered only to deceive. For all that was not flesh was irrelevant to man, and all that was important was man's own flesh, his weakness and corruptibility" (53). As if this were not enough, his loneliness and alienation are dramatically underscored by two events. In the blinding smoke at Chysauster he has a hallucinatory moment that seems like "an experience of nothingness, an experience of death." Soon thereafter he sees himself in Fred, the recently retired worker whose women appear more like keepers than companions. The combination of occurrences is enough to launch Mr. Stone on his desperate bid to halt his own race toward a useless old age and a meaningless death.

Out of his mind is born the scheme for the Knights Companion, ultimately just another gesture for him, but one that achieves fruition on its own merits and leaves him no better off than he was before. Ironically Bill Whymper, who makes nothing, but makes something out of nothing by "licking things into shape," garners all the credit, and Mr. Stone has to resign himself to obscurity. "So impotently ... he raged, and could tell Margaret nothing of what he felt. He feared to make himself ridiculous, and he feared Margaret's impatience: ... So at last the brilliance dimmed, and all that remained was this anxiety, anger and sense of loss" (125-26). Mr. Stone may rage internally, but Naipaul deftly arranges it so that his protagonist's struggle is reflected in several aspects of outer reality. As he notices his reflexes and his mental alertness degenerate, Mr. Stone observes one by one the most familiar components of his surroundings drop away from him, and in their fate he sees his own. First his friend Tony dies, then Miss Millington becomes so decrepit it is obvious that she will have to be released, and finally the old black cat is exterminated. Again, quite understandably it occurs to him that "all that was important was man's own frailty and corruptibility." Alienated from the universe, he begins to feel that destruction is the only order, that man can assert himself by destroying rather than creating.

This mood may at first glance appear out of character for one who up until this point has been so unassertive, but if it is viewed as I think it should be as a culmination of the overpowering egotism which has permeated everything the protagonist does, it will fit into proper place. Mr. Stone lives "sufficient unto himself" for sixty-two years before he secures a mate to flatter him. He is a little man who has fantasies of flying nonchalantly over the heads of ordinary men; and he measures out his life not with coffee spoons (as does Eliot's Prufrock) but by the natural seasons, rather presumptive on his part.

Shortly, however, Mr. Stone descends to his normal plane. Finding in the offspring of the old cat a symbol of renewal that satisfies his need for assurance that "we too would have our spring," he takes a stoic consolation in simply having survived. In a manner similar to that of Biswas, he finally discovers a steady faith that allows him to meet his fate calmly.

It should be noted in comparing the endings to this novel and *A House for Mr Biswas* that there is a notable emphasis placed on human perseverance. Mr. Stone's world is darker than Mr. Biswas', and it marks the growing somberness of Naipaul's dominant tone, but in spite of the physical suffering and defeat of these men they rise in the end above their predicaments. In view of the stresses on continual suffering and the obvious hints that more problems lie ahead, the novels could not be classified as optimistic, but they indicate that there is a way for men to succeed in this absurd life.

VI *The "Hollow Men"*

With certain modifications, what is being said of these two books can be applied to *The Mimic Men, A Flag on the Island,* and *In a Free State.* Human tenacity is still important in Naipaul's next three novels, but the respective endings are progressively more negative as the spiritual rewards for perseverance become rather dubious. The lives of Ralph Singh, Frank, and Bobby are studies in disillusionment. Any positive lessons

to be had from them must be read into the novels. Like Eliot's
hollow men, they exemplify the decadence and emptiness consequent upon living inauthentically in a world which, for no
discernible reason, has come to appear devoid of meaning. It
may be that Ralph Singh is about to come to terms with himself and existence in the final scenes of his story, but Frank and
Bobby obviously are nowhere near a solution. The tone darkens
to the verge of despair.

Without unduly stressing the implications, it is worthwhile
to note that *The Mimic Men* and *A Flag on the Island* appear
after Naipaul has made two rather scathingly severe analyses of
West and East Indian societies in *The Middle Passage* (1962)
and *An Area of Darkness* (1964). Much valid support can be
found for the argument that his ulterior motive in the fiction
is to continue his denunciation of what he dislikes in Trinidad
and India, but too many critics have allowed his explicit statements to distract them from the primary texts which should be
their foremost concern. Within the novels themselves, there is
artistic purpose enough to explain their existence. At one point
in *The Mimic Men*, Naipaul even has his protagonist indicate
the proper terms for any essential comparisons that should be
made. Ralph Singh comments on his autobiography:

I find I have indeed been describing the youth and early manhood of
a leader of some sort, a politician, or at least a disturber. I have
established his isolation, his complex hurt and particular frenzy.
And I believe I have also established, perhaps in this proclaimed
frivolity, this lack of judgement and balance, the deep feeling of
irrelevance and intrusion, his unsuitability for the role into which
he was drawn, and his inevitable failure. From playacting to disorder: it is the pattern. (220)

The hero is pointing his accusing finger at himself, drawing conclusions which are based on his own experience. It is to the
record of his experiences only, to the novel, that critics need
look to determine the author's "purpose."

The autobiographical structuring of *The Mimic Men* and *A
Flag on the Island* has a definite influence over the presentation
of characters, but Naipaul's favorite devices still come into
frequent use; they are simply accommodated to the personalities

of the protagonists. Ralph Singh displays a propensity to generalize about groups according to nationalities, and as for individuals he picks out typical gestures and eccentricities by which to label and remember them. Such "tagging" makes the description of people appear one-sided, but in this book Naipaul has his narrator aware of their flatness. According to his philosophy, people who come to the city lose much of their identity. "In the great city, so three-dimensional, so rooted in its soil, drawing colour from such depths, only the city was real. Those of us who came to it lost some of our solidity; we were trapped into fixed, flat postures" (32). In another place the very nature of his terminology exposes the dehumanized quality of his relationships. "After some time the body threw me off, rearranging its stiff, evil-smelling hair" (34). His partner in this sexual encounter is treated as a thing, the neuter pronoun and the anonymity of "body" expressing his disgust far more eloquently than any amount of elaborate description could have.

There are also frequent "characters." In *The Mimic Men*, Hoc plays up his nervousness, Cecil his recklessness; Browne assumes the stereotype of the comic Negro, then later exchanges it for the "radical" black leader. Ralph's father gains a reputation as a cafe wrecker but changes into a mystical religious leader, "Gurudeva," and moves to the hills. In *A Flag on the Island*, there is Mano who cannot win walking races because he always ends up running, Mr. Lambert who sells his concocted brew at sporting events, and H. J. B. White, a black man who leaves off imitating Jane Austen's style and exploits the demand in white countries for black "hate" literature. *In a Free State* contains the stock figure of the irascible old colonial diehard, "the colonel."

At the same time, each of these novels contains effective passages of dialogue which contribute much to the exposition of character. Sections of *The Mimic Men*, especially those dealing with Ralph's island childhood, contain good examples; but the same color and power of dialect from the early novels fill the pages of *A Flag on the Island*. It takes Priest only a second to change from sorrow to anger when he learns that Ma Ho, who has just died shortly after taking out an insurance policy, had duped him by submitting a bogus urine specimen to pass his physical examination.

"Was not his pee," Henry said. "That was why he didn't want to
go to the doctor. That was why he wanted the doctor to come to *him*."
"O God!" Priest said. "O God! The Chinese bitch. He make me
lose my bonus. And you, Henry. You black like me and you didn't
tell me nothing. You see," he said to the room, "why black people
don't progress in this place. No corporation."

"Some people corporate in one way," Henry said, "Some people
corporate in another way." (203)

Obviously the lost bonus takes precedence over the lost life when
the trick is exposed. Such lighthearted exchanges in an otherwise
predominantly depressing novel are welcome relief. They fit
nicely into the context of the book, however, because they blend
with the fatalistic type of humor that comes with the protagonist's mood.

Thus, in both of these works as in *Mr Stone and the Knights
Companion*, an outstanding feature of Naipaul's characterization and style involves the subordination of all minor figures to
the controlling influence of the heroes' personalities. Artistic
grounds to support the consistency of this sort of subordination
are not far to seek in the psychological makeup of either Ralph
Singh or Frank. Both of them express a feeling which might be
termed a "rage for order." In Ralph I have already pointed out
a tendency to view people as two-dimensional; whether they
actually are this way is not germane; this is the way he sees
them, and he is consequently unable to get behind the exteriors
they present, to the basic humanity beneath. Instead he endeavors to relate to them as though they are flat, posturing
characters in a vast drama. It is significant that on occasion he
refers to the "cinematic blur" of his childhood, the "drama" that
he and others are enacting and the "celestial camera" which records his every movement for an audience in whose existence
he does not believe. In all that he does he is sensitive to a conviction of fraudulence. He assumes roles, most usually that of
the "dandy," but he fails to discover his authentic selfhood.

His own explanation for his personal failure is couched in
terms of his disconcerting stint as a colonial politician.

The pace of events, as I see it, is no more than the pace of a chaos
on which strict limits have been imposed. I speak of course of terri-

tories like Isabella, set adrift yet not altogether abandoned, where this controlled chaos approximates in the end . . . to a continuing order. The chaos lies all within.

I will not linger on the details of our movement. I cannot speak of the movement as a phenomenon generated by my personality. I can scarcely speak of it in personal terms. The politician deals in abstractions, even when he deals with himself. He is a man lifted out of himself and separate from his personality, which he ought to acknowledge from time to time. (230)

It so happens that his current situation, exile in a foreign country, is the direct result of political chaos, but the obvious political causes behind his expatriation and personal dislocation are at best only secondary. Deeper within lies a basic dissatisfaction, an alienation that has plagued him since youth. No matter how true it may be that his short public career fits a common pattern, the important fact remains that he has never felt at home anywhere or at any time in his life.

From early youth his native island impresses him as a place of shipwreck. Often he indulges in reveries about his Aryan ancestors, magnificent horsemen wandering the Himalayan mountains in search of him, their lost chieftain. In his fantasies he rejects Isabella's sea and sand and imagines that his true native environment is mountains and snow.

When he finally exchanges his tropical Isabella for temperate London, his rootless isolation is merely transplanted to another setting.

In the city as nowhere else we are reminded that we are individuals, units. . . .

So quickly had London gone sour on me. The great city, centre of the world, in which, fleeing disorder, I had hoped to find the beginning of order. So much had been promised by the physical aspect. (22)

As his experiences make more and more clear, he is not to find the order he seeks in physical appearances. In London he undertakes the "romance of interracial marriage" with Sandra, who is just as lost as he is. On the island they play at making money and attempt to lose themselves in the social whirl. Then Ralph is caught up increasingly with the accelerating game of island politics. In each of these endeavors the basic falsity soon results in more disorder: the marriage ends in divorce; the pleasure bought with money fades; the social circle disintegrates into quarreling factions; the political charade falls apart. Ultimately, the mimicry out of which he attempts to fashion an organized, meaningful existence leads to disillusionment and frenzy.

Lacking the ability to impose any controlling direction on life, he decides to withdraw from it. He gives up both the ideal fantasies of his youth and the ineffectual posturings which mark his later activities.

I no longer dream of ideal landscapes or seek to attach myself to them. All landscapes eventually turn to land, the gold of the imagination to the lead of the reality. . . . I could not pretend even to myself to be part of a community or to be putting down roots. I prefer the freedom of my far-out suburban hotel, the absence of responsibility; I like the feeling of impermanence. (13-14)

Freed from external pressures in retirement, he at last settles upon a method of establishing order. With detachment and restored calm he takes up his pen and, turning to the past, assembles the fragments of his shattered experiences into an intelligible whole. The result of his effort is his representative autobiographical sketch, the story of *The Mimic Men.*

If the narrative tone is rather static, the protagonist cool and detached, the action described as often as it is portrayed, and the point of view restrictive, before these items may be leveled justly as criticism against the novel, the fictional situation created for its presentation must be carefully examined. More dramatic action and a broader, more varied perspective might be preferred by some, but the terms upon which the book is structured conform to a different pattern. In order to reveal the character of a man who is suspended without a meaningful existence between worlds to which he is unable to relate, Naipaul has chosen to allow the speaker to express himself in conformity with the type of person that he is. Ralph Singh is detached and philosophical, and he has arrived at this serene state only after exasperating years of fruitless involvement in pointless activity. He sees his case as somewhat typical of colonial existence; he is uprooted and lacks both the knowledge and the means to work out his own order; he has to borrow, to mimic the examples which have been set for him by others. The result is restlessness and disorder; and it is to combat this that he finally withdraws from life and undertakes writing. His first intention is to record the unnatural falsity and disorientation of colonial living in general, but as he confesses, "I am too much a victim of that restlessness which was to have been my subject. And it must also be confessed that in that dream of writing I was attracted less by the act and the labour than by the calm and the order which the act would have implied" (38-39). His "rage for order," then, drives him finally into himself; it is there that he must reach a still, calm center. It is there, too, that we must look to reach a proper understanding of his narrative.

It is significant that around the "active" part of his life he decides to place parentheses. This is the symbolic gesture he makes to create the semblance of order which has eluded him from the beginning. His story, even in the disclosures of his early youth, is not intended to be highly dramatized; he wishes to be analytical as well as expository in putting things in their proper place. The resultant form has the effect of montage wherein dream, reality, and documentary comment blend smoothly and evenly.

Turning from *The Mimic Men* to *A Flag on the Island*, it appears that character and style undergo little change. Local color is prominent here, but the controlling atmosphere of the story derives from the narrator's frame of mind. Frank is motivated by the same frenzied desire for order that drives Ralph. In Frank's case, however, his problem is not so much a lack of order as a rejection of the one that exists. As is evident from his disdain for names, labels, the new flag, and other signs of the foreign standardization that is sweeping the island, he too directs his rage toward fraud and inauthenticity. In graduated stages of despair he races about the once familiar island in an effort to rediscover the lost reality that he remembers. "In my moods I tell myself that the world is not being washed away; that there is time; that the blurring of fantasy with reality which gives me the feeling of helplessness exists only in my mind. But then I know that the mind is alien and unfriendly, and I am never able to regulate things. Hilton, Hilton. Even here, even in the book on the bedside table" (158). His account displays the same concern for theatrics that stands out in Ralph's story. The "blurring of fantasy and reality" is quite literal. Comic "tag" names such as Bippy, Chippy, and Tippy from "Foundationland" and the stylized final scenes where reality fades into stage setting and then defines itself again are logically consistent with the mental state of the narrator.

In *In a Free State*, as in the last two novels, the landscape tends to lose its distinctness at times. Place descriptions occur, but a sense of unreality enters Bobby's perception just as it has Ralph's and Frank's. Only slightly less self-consciously than Ralph, Bobby also experiences the feeling that he is performing a part, that he is involved in a drama. It becomes increasingly obvious that Naipaul's main concern is not with reality just as it might appear in a photograph but as it is perceived by his heroes. In depicting their introverted conceptualizations, he has certainly individualized each one, but he has also concentrated on certain basic aspects that make them identical with mankind elsewhere.

It has been argued that in thus universalizing his presentation, Naipaul has damaged his sense of realism and has, in effect, gone the route of other self-exiled West Indian writers who critics say have lost essential contact with the most familiar source of their material.[19] But in answer to this criticism I submit that there are valid grounds within the novels themselves to account at least partially for the "vagueness" and "distance" that critics have heretofore attributed to a fault in Naipaul's art. The protagonist's disengagement from the narrative strand can under certain circumstances be an asset rather than a liability. Ironic humor in the early novels and the detached, analytical tone of the later ones prevent the reader from becoming deeply involved in the stories, but at the same time they yield valuable insights into the personalities of the different protagonists. These devices may be viewed as defensive mechanisms which are just as much a part of character as any other trait. If it were a matter of the absence of concreteness and dramatic tension, then certainly the novels would be severely damaged; but this is not the case. Realism and verisimilitude are maintained at a high level of accuracy even when the view is of a mental landscape. There is truth in Frank's assertion, "all landscapes are in the end only in the imagination."

CHAPTER 4

Dominant Attitudes

I *Motive for Humor*

N AIPAUL'S most prevalent attitude is satirical. Certain parts of his works fall into the category of satire under both of the usual definitions of the genre. His first four novels, especially with their colorful mixture and variety, make a "full plate, a medley"; and time after time throughout all his books, in action, character, setting and theme he employs his incisive wit to hold up to ridicule the foibles and follies of man and society. "The final test for satire is the typical emotion which the author feels, and wishes to evoke in his readers. It is a blend of amusement and contempt. In some satirists, the amusement far outweighs the contempt. In others it almost disappears: it changes into a sour sneer, or a grim smile, or a wry awareness that life cannot all be called reasonable or noble."[1]

Should there be any doubt after reading the novels as to Naipaul's desire to evoke amused contempt, unmistakable proof of his intent is to be had in his explicit remarks concerning the corrective and formative values of satire. In the section on Trinidad in *The Middle Passage* he discusses at length the tasteless, materialistic, uncreative, imitative West Indian middle class and the narrow, race-and-color-blinded writer of the area who "has not only failed to diagnose the sickness of his society but has aggravated it" (70). He contends that no one has adequately decried the falsity at the heart of the Trinidadian's way of life, his frustrated attempt to identify with foreign values.

It is not easy to write about the West Indian middle class. The most exquisite gifts of irony and perhaps malice would be required to keep the characters from slipping into an unremarkable mid-Atlantic whiteness. They would have to be treated as real people with real problems and responsibilities and affections—and this has been done—but they would also have to be treated as people whose lives have been corrupted by a fantasy which is their cross. (69)

Recognizing the need, he doubts the likelihood of its being met under existing conditions. There appears to be a lack of maturity on the part of writers, an inability to develop the "gifts of subtlety and brutality" that are necessary to attack extant problems. "Improvement begins with the recognition of difference; it begins with the direct vision and the compassion of a Chekhov or a Dickens."[2]

In a sense, what Naipaul is asking for is the same kind of mature detachment that is mentioned in the conclusion of the previous chapter. At least the appearance of aloofness and perhaps callousness will attach itself to the writer who manages to disengage himself from his native environment to the extent that he can turn upon it, dissect it, and come to grips with its fundamental weaknesses. Naipaul is usually successful in maintaining distance from his material, but contrary to the objections of such men as George Lamming and A. C. Derrick, this does not necessarily mean that he is coldly detached or disdainful of that which he is depicting.[3] Rather, his concerted effort to remove himself and his failure at times to keep his personal feelings hidden are evidence of his deeply rooted attachment to the people he criticizes. "Naipaul has consciously invoked comedy in order to say something deeply and seriously felt about a social predicament." Moreover, "we must bear in mind that Naipaul is writing about an idiosyncratic society, a real society about which he feels considerable worry and concern."[4]

His expressed motive is not unlike that of most satirists of the past who claim a serious purpose, but also as with some of his predecessors the weight of humor indicates that at least at times he is simply indulging in sheer fun. In the lighter, early novels this is especially so, yet it extends on into the somber later period. His usual method echoes that practiced before him by such masters of comic grotesquerie as Washington Irving and Charles Dickens. After their example, too, the vehicles of his satire, characters and narrators alike, assume lives of their own so that they never degenerate into mere tools. As a matter of fact, dramatization of their existence is so absorbing that the specific objects of his thrusts are effectively screened and constitute only a part of the larger action. The beauty of his muted satire is that it merges almost indiscernibly with the overall humor of the books.

There appear to be approximately three levels on which the humor functions. First are the jokes, pranks, and laughter-provoking incidents which occur among the characters. Second come eccentricities, language, and actions the humor of which is not always consciously felt by narrators and participants within the stories. On this level dramatic irony comes into prominence since the reader's position allows him fuller appreciation of meanings unavailable to the characters. Third is the sophisticated level on which the objects of satire come into sharper focus. Between these there are no gaps or boundaries; they are complementary, only gradations of emphasis marking them as closer to one end of the scale or the other.

II *The Literal Phase*

The most literal phase, wherein the quality of humor is accommodated to the people who are joking and playing tricks on one another, has rather limited possibilities for use. It is a mark of Naipaul's comic style that his amusing comedy emerges through his characters' individual dispositions and the thoughts they utter rather than through situation. All that they do helps to reveal their personalities, but it is not until the latter part of *Miguel Street* and in *A House for Mr Biswas* that he succeeds in deriving multiple values out of what previously had amounted to little more than funny remarks and incidents.

Examples of the early practice are illustrated throughout *The Mystic Masseur* by the narrator, by minor characters, and by the protagonist. The narrator offers a damning apology for quack doctors who his mother says "think nothing of killing two three people before breakfast." He explains, "This wasn't as bad as it sounds: in Trinidad the midday meal is called breakfast" (7). At the kedgeree ceremony the crowd chides Ramlogan for not offering Ganesh enough dowry. "Give the boy money, man. What you think he sitting down there for? To take out

his photo?" (51). Ganesh extracts a clever sexual twist from
Leela's inclination to fall asleep whenever he reads to her.

"Can't help it, man. The moment you start reading to me you
does make me feel sleepy. I know some people does feel sleepy the
moment they see a bed."
"They is people with clean mind." (79)

The Suffrage of Elvira offers similar examples. Baksh directs
humor at himself by emphasizing his failure to draw many votes
in the general election. Sexual innuendo does not elicit laughter,
but it displays Ramlogan's biting wit when he taunts Chittaranjan
about his daughter's conduct. "When girl children small, they
does crawl, as the saying goes. Then they does start walking.
Then they does lie down. As the saying goes. Ain't something
I sit down and invent" (123). These kinds of expressions extend
into Miguel Street, but they are often accompanied by qualify-
ing, thoughtful passages. The young narrator cannot bring himself to participate in laughing at Big Foot's cowardice, Morgan's
compulsive clowning, or Hat's pathetic attempt at mirth before
the judge. In scenes such as those where he jests mildly with
his mother and his uncle Bhakcu about his leaving the island,
there is a definite undertone of sympathy that has not come to
the surface in the two prior novels.

The direction indicated in Miguel Street becomes more prominent in A House for Mr Biswas. Mr. Biswas often assumes the
role of the clown. At the Tulsis' he takes malicious delight in
coining derogatory epithets for the members of Shama's family:
Mrs. Tulsi is "the old hen," Seth the "Big Boss," Owad and
Shekhar "the young gods," Hari "the constipated holy man" or
"the holy ghost." But more often than not his pranks return to
haunt him. Seth labels him "Biswas the paddler" because he
wants to paddle his own canoe rather than pitch his lot with
the family. And his infantile dumping of food on Owad results
in a humiliating beating. As time goes by, his facetiousness
begins to burden him considerably. The weight of his personal
discomfort is only intensified as he sees those around him drawn
into his own transgressions. His family suffers; Shama is pres-
sured into destroying the lovely dollhouse he imprudently gives
to Savi; the children have to bear the "little paddler" label; and

at one point his folly almost results in Anand's death. At a swimming party while Mr. Biswas inadvertently becomes the victim of his own clowning, his son, unattended, nearly drowns. Mr. Biswas attempts to make light of his son's distress, but the pain he tries to conceal behind a grinning exterior is registered unmistakably by the increasing amount of stomach powder he has to consume.

Thus, in his fourth novel, Naipaul's use of humor even on the elementary level grows significantly more penetrating. The consequences of "innocent" fun are shown to be extensive and often painful, and they begin to bear more directly on the novel's overall development. The result of his changing strategy is marked by his growing seriousness and the noticeable reduction in the number and frequency of scenes containing farcical elements. It should be noted that in *Mr Stone and the Knights Companion* the protagonist's only successful joke is at his own expense and is purely unintentional on his part. His forgetting that it is mice and not cats that eat cheese makes his elaborate arrangements to entrap the black cat appear ridiculous. When Mr. Stone tells of his scheme, however, he finds enjoyment in the sympathetic interest that it arouses. Mrs. Springer's reiteration of his tale "was for him a new sensation; he luxuriated in it" (17). Unfortunately his newfound pleasure trips him up with overconfidence; his banal pun—"you are anxious to get me under the affluence of incohol" (14)—had previously met with the embarrassed silence it deserves. But, encouraged by Mrs. Springer's approval, he attempts a witty play on the similarity between walnuts and brains and fares even more miserably than before. Such is the subdued level of humor throughout the novel, depressingly pathetic gestures which reflect the insecurity and insipidity of Mr. Stone's existence.

Though portions of *The Mimic Men, A Flag on the Island,* and *In a Free State* recall something of the lightness of the early novels, they reflect a deeper seriousness of expression. Hoc and Ralph Singh as children could create laughter by exaggerating their "nervous" eating habits by consuming collars, ties, and pages from books, but as an older man Ralph has come to the conclusion that we never merely play: "As though we ever play. As though the personality, for all its byways and wilful devia-

tions, all its seeming inconsistencies, does not hang together"
(31). He, Hoc, Cecil, his father could play at being "characters"
and could pretend that their island was absurdly funny, but in
so doing they were creating an artificial world. "Anything that
touched on everyday life excited laughter when it was mentioned in a classroom: the name of a shop, the name of a street,
the name of street-corner foods. The laughter denied our
knowledge of these things to which after the hours of school
we were to return" (114). Ralph's father might joke about
sabotaging the Coca Cola plant he detests by placing a dead
mouse in their vats, but the reality of the plant as the reality
of the undesirable everyday world continues to survive these
denials unscathed.

III *Emerging Irony*

More often than not, in keeping with the various characters'
moods, the humor is tinged with deeper meanings. Browne,
a black man, is permitted his racial slur against the body odor
of his supporters, "the old *bouquet d'Afrique.*" Such jokes are
simply not very funny; nor are they apparently intended to be.
Naipaul conditions them to fit the personalities of the people
he is portraying. Special difficulties attach to his more complex
technique, because at times it is impossible to distinguish the
limits of the character's awareness. For example, in *A Flag on
the Island* it is not made clear whether Selma recognizes the
depths of banality revealed in her bathroom decorations; but
Frank's repulsion deftly underscores his expressed dislike for
all the gross modernity of her house.

The mat said RESERVED FOR DRIPS. On the lavatory seat there was
a notice, flowers painted among the words: GENTLEMEN LIFT THE
SEAT IT IS SHORTER THAN YOU THINK LADIES REMAIN SEATED THROUGH-
OUT THE PERFORMANCE. An ashtray; a little book of lavatory and
bedroom jokes. The two so often going together. Poor Selma. (230)

At moments of deeper consciousness such as this, which
abound in the last three novels, the first and second levels on
which humor operates imperceptibly merge with each other.
To a great extent, the main characters, because the world being

presented is largely the world of their perception, share almost the same degree of insight that we might normally expect to be available only to the author and reader. This is not to say that esthetic distance is violated, but in a sense it is a compliment to the special quality of verisimilitude that is typical of Naipaul's later fiction. The effect is obtained, not by the vehicle of an omniscient narrator, but rather by the presentation of fictional men who are affected much as any acutely sensitive person would be in the given situation. Unlike poor Mr. Stone, such men as Ralph, Frank, and Bobby can appreciate a bad pun for what it is. Frank's more adept facility with word play bears comparison with Mr. Stone's ineffectual jokes. As Selma takes him to bed she attempts to assuage his anger. "Come. Be good." But he twists her straight line to fit the sexual context. "I will be good if I come" (229). Even when he slips and utters a cliché—"What makes a girl like you come to a place like this?" (178)—he recognizes the meanness of the implication and is immediately ashamed. The difference between his reaction and Mr. Stone's is his ability to recover his poise quickly and move forward.

The increasing awareness of the heroes from Mr. Biswas through Bobby has a direct influence on the grade of the humor and its treatment; it tends to become carefully modulated wit, with subtle ironic tones interwoven. Bobby and Linda laugh little, smile sardonically over the blindness and inconsistencies of people closest to them. This urbane attitude reflects a superficial complacency, but at the same time it reveals the ennui of their lives. Bobby tries for humor in alluding to the colonel's body odor. "I thought only Africans smelled. What is it that Doris Marshall says? That little bit of settler wisdom about civilization and cleanliness?" (214). Linda attempts to ignore at first, then tears appear beneath her dark glasses. She overcomes her sentiment, but for a moment this personal confrontation with the "white man's burden" is depressing.

Though it is a factor, standard dramatic irony plays only a minor part in the humor of the last three novels. From the outside we are enabled to observe the apocalyptic, perhaps the absurd, nature of the frenzied events preceding the hurricane in *A Flag on the Island*, but to a great extent Frank, too, is alert to the fantastic aspect of the situation. Priest's televised diatribe, the wild dancing, the unexpected but predictable discovery that Leonard is insane, and the theatrical quality of Blackwhite's pursuit by the Foundationlanders are all patent grotesqueries, and even while he is caught in the midst of them the narrator recognizes them as such. Just as his earlier endeavors to help people get what they say they want eventually ruins the island for him, he cannot remedy the state of affairs, but at least he understands his complicity in them.

In *The Mimic Men*, Ralph Singh's protracted intellectual detachment makes it easier to distinguish between the first two levels of Naipaul's humor. The narrator in most instances is one step removed from the scenes he describes, explaining and comparing them. Thus, he disassociates himself from events which in the earlier novels incline toward burlesque. Dialect jokes, eccentric characters, and buffoonery are not left to themselves but are accompanied by his personal reactions. Laughter is not directed at Rudolfo because of his strange dialect but because of the kind of confusion that results from his mispronunciation of "a sheet of paper." In asking for what he wants he mistakenly gives the short "i" rather than the proper long "e" sound and consequently gets a roll of toilet tissue.[5] Evidence of the characters' sophistication is contained in the fact that at least some of them are cognizant of the language problem and have arrived at a position where they can enjoy their superiority over their past.

This kind of perception for the most part eludes Mr. Stone, who does not appear to be able fully to comprehend the things that happen to him, much less their comic aspects. His life has been too long uneventful and unimaginative. "He knew that puns were in bad taste, though he didn't know exactly why" (15). What humor there is is usually wasted on him and the other characters, and for the reader consists primarily in a pleasurable recognition of the piquant gestures and weaknesses that are skillfully drawn out of their personalities. Probably the best adjective to describe the Stones' first dinner party is "lugubrious." While Margaret entertains the women in one room, Mr. Stone and the men wait uncomfortably in another. As we learn, Tomlinson might have attempted a dirty story, but his last effort had been told so meticulously that it had fallen flat, "no one knowing when it had ended, no one laughing, everyone embarrassed and slightly shocked, for without wit the story had appeared only as a piece of wilful obscenity" (49).

Mr. Biswas partakes of the deeper insights typical of Ralph Singh and Frank, and consequently the range of humor in *A House for Mr Biswas* is more extensive than it is in *Mr Stone and the Knights Companion*. This large book contains early signs of Naipaul's growing seriousness, but it also exhibits some of the lighter comedy of the early novels. "If he [Mr. Biswas] resembles some of the grotesques of Dickens, he has been created by a writer who has a more contemporary sense of the themes of void, loneliness, meaninglessness and absurdity, so prevalent in modern European literature."[6] In addition to his own clowning, which is often merely to cover for his innermost feelings, he is made the unwilling and sometimes unsuspecting object of humor.

An excellent example of the way his lively imagination plays with his sober thought patterns occurs in his first visit to the offices of the *Trinidad Sentinel*. As he carries on a normal conversation with the receptionist, fragmentary newspaper headings keep flashing through his mind. The violence he represses as he attempts to answer her obnoxious questions expresses itself in terms of a sensational news item which assumes form as they talk.

> *Amazing scenes were witnessed in St. Vincent Street yesterday when Mohun Biswas, 31 . . .*
> "You got an appointment?"
> *. . . assaulted a receptionist*
> "No," Mr Biswas said irritably.
> *In an interview with our reporter . . .* (288)

The story ends in blazing guns, mass murder, and fire. In this instance, the protagonist molds his own private comedy. He appears more of a victim as the builder of his house at Green Vale dryly accepts each reduction in the scale of the project, and in the way he allows his sense of propriety to keep him from looking critically at the jerry-built house he eventually buys on Sikkim Street. As he remains silent, thinking guiltily of how his hidden poverty is deceiving the hospitable solicitor's clerk, the price drops from six thousand dollars. " 'Five five and we will throw in this morris suite.' The clerk gave a little laugh. 'I always hear that Indians was sharp bargainers, but I never know till now just how sharp they was' " (509). Ironically, as Mr. Biswas discovers after it is too late, not only is the house poorly built but he could have gotten a better one for much less money. In other parts of the book—when he is mocked by the laborers at Green Vale, when he imitates Mrs. Tulsi by providing "brain food" for Anand, and when he is depicted as anxiously kicking out behind him to disperse the "readers and learners" from around Miss Logie's automobile—he simply looks foolish.

In this last respect Mr. Biswas is an obvious descendant of figures from the earlier novels. Naipaul plays lightly upon his several eccentricities and then touches upon their roots in his deeper emotions, just as he begins to do at places in *Miguel Street*. But in the first three books there seems to be a proportionally greater amount of humor which is at the expense of the characters rather than in sympathy with them. Thus on the secondary level in these works, we are frequently placed in a position to laugh at people and their activities. Exaggeration is unmistakable in the comparative description of the Mrs. Bhakcu and Morgan. "Mrs. Bhakcu was four feet high, three feet wide, and three feet deep. Mrs. Morgan was a little over six foot tall and built like a weight-lifter" (81-82). The disparity is made even more ludicrous by the manner in which the smaller woman castigates and threatens the larger across their adjoining fences. Bhakcu is a good match for his wife. Trapped beneath the car on which he has been working, he forgets his helpless position and abuses Hat, who has come to his rescue.

"Hat," Bhakcu shouted from under the car, "the moment you get this car from off me, I going to break up your tail."
"Man," Mrs. Bhakcu said to her husband, "how you so advantageous? The man come round with his good good mind to help you and now you want to beat him up?"
Hat began to look hurt and misunderstood. (148)

Scenes such as these are delightfully funny and blend into
the scheme of the book, but they are also indicative of the
lightness of Naipaul's technique. At this point, the humor does
not contribute much more than amusement to the overall work.
It is rather significant that in *Miguel Street* the author (through
his ingenuous narrator) apparently feels it necessary to point
up the suffering that frequently underlies laughter by balancing
the less weighty passages with reflective pauses for serious
thought. "The laughter of Miguel Street is sometimes crude and
cynical. But whenever this occurs, the boy points out the need
for a greater sensitivity. . . . There are the several occasions
when Hat threatens to thrash Boysie [*sic*] if he dares laugh at
the latest Miguel Street misfortune."[7]

With the inclusion of these serious moments, however, as an
advancement over *The Suffrage of Elvira* and *The Mystic Masseur*
there is at least a conscious effort to balance and weigh the
"farcical" aspects of the work. The usage of humor on the second
level is especially noticeable in Naipaul's first two novels. The
reader is afforded a view not only of the characters' own colorful
games and tricks ˗but also of their less conscious quirks of
gesture, dress, and language that, because of their incongruity,
are highly entertaining. As "characters" they cultivate various
eccentricities and Naipaul reveals the ludicrous aspects of their
words and actions.

In *The Mystic Masseur,* Naipaul plays upon their delightful
vagaries of dialect. Leela, probably influenced by Ganesh's
abortive attempt to purify their tongue and make it good
English, affects a grammar all her own to go along with her
increasing refinement. "She used a private accent which softened
all harsh vowel sounds; her grammar owed nothing to anybody,
and included a highly personal conjugation of the verb to be"
(150). But in this first novel the overall language structure
contains an even more interesting comic device. Mock-heroic
elements begin to appear when in the first chapter the narrator
makes the pompous claim that "the history of Ganesh is, in a
way, the history of our times" (14). They become more definite
as the speaker meticulously corroborates his inflated estimations
with pseudoauthentic data from the masseur's published works
and as he carefully underscores unimportant events that conceal

portents of the future. A. C. Derrick singles out the scene wherein Ganesh heals Leela's foot, but there are many instances where the narrator's pretentious acceptance of things at face value makes his commentary appear "sardonic, and accentuates the sort of mock heroic terms of portrayal in the novel."[8]

Without resorting to the usual paraphernalia of classical mock epics, in fact with eloquent simplicity and straightforwardness Naipaul treats a trivial figure in an overblown style so that his subject becomes ridiculous. The mystic masseur is said to be one of the most important men in the Caribbean—he is important enough to be mentioned in Naipaul's next two novels. As it turns out, however, not only is his career a fluke, but he is a charlatan, a political opportunist, and a bitter, disillusioned man. The ironic point, and the point that turns Naipaul's humor into poignant satire, is that this paramount fraud is respected and venerated by the "picaroon" society out of which he grows, the very society, by the way, which populates all but two of Naipaul's novels.

IV The Satirical Phase

Thus, the third of the levels, the satirical, is founded upon the first two and derives its humorous thrust from them. To state the case in its broadest terms, Naipaul holds up to ridicule several of the distasteful and irrational aspects of man and his institutions. More specifically (according to his own statements), he is concerned variously with "fantasy," "corruption," and "sickness." He begins with a recognition of the gross difference between the situation as he finds it and his conception of an ideal, and in order to draw attention to the discrepancy he selectively elaborates upon those things which he finds to be trivial, repellent, or otherwise contemptible.

With the introduction of politics near the end of his first book, he hits upon an excellent theme which affords opportunities to explore the less than admirable goals not only of individuals but of the whole community. As the stories of Ganesh and Harbans make abundantly clear, the motivation for advancement is largely materialistic. Baksh informs Harbans as to what newly established democracy means to the voters.

"What you say about 1946 is true. Nobody did spend much money. But that was only the fust election. People did just go and vote for the man they like. Now is different. People learning. You have to spend on them."

"Yes you have to spend on them," Dhaniram said, his legs shaking, his eyes dancing. He relished all the grand vocabulary of the election. "Otherwise somebody else going to spend on them." (51)

Harbans' only consolation is the prospect of abundant repayment after he takes office. As a matter of fact, what little influence he has with the government before the election he is already turning to personal advantage on road repairs.

Minor details such as this indicate the nature of these men and subtly dramatize Naipaul's indictment elsewhere of the middle-class concept of respectability. "I knew Trinidad to be unimportant, uncreative, cynical. . . . Power was recognized, but dignity was allowed to no one. Every person of eminence was held to be crooked and contemptible. We lived in a society which denied itself heroes."[9] This external reference should not be interpreted as an argument in support of the author's "intention"; on the contrary, I am in agreement with David Ormerod's conclusion: "It would seem . . . that Naipaul deliberately avoids the depiction of communal confrontation in order to create 'literature' (which is universal) and avoid 'propaganda' (which is rooted in a special situation)."[10] I merely wish to indicate the recognizable coincidence of thought that exists between the two separate methods of expression. Naipaul's satire is "topical" in the sense that all satire must be topical if it is to be pertinent. But in keeping with the best tradition, his work touches upon events that are easily translatable into universal terms. After all, political opportunism and crassly imitative picaroon societies are not inventions of the emerging Third World.

In a way it is true, as the narrator of *The Mystic Masseur* suggests, that the history of Ganesh is a history of the times. The characters are all in favor of improvement, but they have not yet adapted to the changes that are overtaking them. This is skillfully revealed at the governor's dinner party. Coming to the formal meal are colorful representatives of most of the island's heterogeneous population; and from the variegated costumes through the several breaches of etiquette to Mr. Primrose's unoriginal dropping of his monocle into the soup, there is one humiliating *faux pas* after another. "The meal was torture to Ganesh. He felt alien and uncomfortable. He grew sulkier and sulkier and refused all the courses. He felt as if he were a boy again, going to the Queen's Royal College for the first time" (204).

The final thrust of the first novel is in the ironic change that comes over the masseur. In spite of his well-intentioned principles, he succumbs to corruption and concedes to the white controllers of his colonial world even his identity, becoming G. Ramsay Muir. The very same problem of psychological disunity rises to the surface again in the highly complex sixth novel, *The Mimic Men*. Social turmoil here too is focused conveniently in the colonial political situation. The narrator's description could hardly be more explicit.

The colonial politician is an easy object of satire. I wish to avoid satire; I will leave out the stories of illiteracy and social innocence. Not that I wish to present him as grander or less flawed than he is. It is that his situation satirizes itself, turns satire inside out, takes satire to a point where it touches pathos if not tragedy. Out of his immense violation words come easily to him, too easily. He must go back on his words. In success he must lay aside violation. He must betray himself and in the end he has no cause save his own survival. The support he has attracted, not ideal to ideal, but bitterness to bitterness, he betrays and mangles: emancipation is not possible for all. (250)

In the end, then, selfishness and self-betrayal undermine the individual who is already rootless in his formless, transitional society.

This same problem, but not in political terms, is developed extensively in *A House for Mr Biswas*. The story of Mr. Biswas' life is of his being "shunted from one decaying hut to another, a microcosm of three hundred years of West Indian history."[11] His struggle for meaningful independence is an admirable one whether he always looks noble or not. His antagonist outside of his own follies and weaknesses is embodied in the closed authoritarian structure of Hanuman House—the internal arrangement of which closely resembles the family pattern described in *The Middle Passage*: "an enclosing self-sufficient world absorbed with its quarrels and jealousies, as difficult for the outsider to penetrate as for one of its members to escape. It protected and imprisoned, a static world, awaiting decay" (81-82). The Tulsi dwelling might easily be taken symbolically as either the ancient conformation of the dying East Indian way of life or as the type of paternal colonialism that begins to be shaken off after World War II. In either respect, the decrepit Tulsi institution is under constant attack by Mr. Biswas because it poses an ambivalent threat to his individuality. He must break away from it or be consumed into nonentity; but to escape is to give up security for an uncertain liberty.

Before he can determine his own fate, however, the dynasty itself begins to break apart. At Shorthills—with the death of the family pundit, Hari, and the gradual loosening of authority consequent upon the widening rift between Mrs. Tulsi and Seth—the old order gives place to a new brand of selfish individualism. "At this point it is clear that the object of Naipaul's satire is changing from a static communalism to the new colonial individualism. This gives a kind of back-flip of sympathy to the old Tulsi way of life (and this is supported by Mr. Biswas's recognition, at times of unbalancing stress, of the protectiveness even of Hanuman House)."[12] Gradually chaos builds as the several branches of the family inconsiderately strike out to better themselves regardless of the consequences to others or of the absurdity of their schemes.

One avenue of advancement, one which receives passing notice in all the novels except *Mr Stone and the Knights Companion,* is education. In *The Mystic Masseur* Suruj Mooma, jealous of Leela's ability to write, makes self-righteous remarks about the harmful effects of modern education. On the other hand, in *Miguel Street,* Elias' futile three-year marathon bout with the sanitary inspector's test gives an indication of the importance of scholastic and technical examinations in schools; for many it represents not just the most desirable but the only escape from poverty.

But because of the system and its questionable method of operation, the public schools receive rather uncomplimentary attention throughout Naipaul's fiction. Ganesh learns that his job as a teacher "is to form, not to inform" (20). Judging from classroom theme assignments cited in *A House for Mr Biswas* and *The Mimic Men,* the lessons are intended to form imitations of middle-class English children. Students learn to call their parents "Mummy and Daddy"; they learn that they are supposed to spend weekends at the beach; and they learn to apply for employment in jobs for which they are unqualified.[13] Probably the most devastatingly incisive satire occurs in the painfully ridiculous scenes following Anand Biswas through his successful scholastic examination. Preparations are so elaborate the boy has more than sufficient cause to complain, "Anybody would believe I am going to this place to get married" (425). In passing the exam, he is able to realize his father's unfulfilled dreams; he is freed from the Tulsis and from the island's debilitating environment.

V *Brunt of the Attack*

From evidence contained in the novels, it appears that what is wrong with the educational system is about the same as what ails the political framework; both foment degrading imitation; both are geared almost exclusively to the achievement of material success; both are utterly lacking in principles which would allow for authentic self-fulfillment. In turn, the effects of these weaknesses are intensified by the social lethargy which permits them to continue unchecked and essentially unquestioned. Naipaul's satire singles out numerous distinguishable targets. In various places he picks at the vulnerability of individuals—charlatans, politicians, missionaries, sensation-seeking journalists, public relations men, tourists—and of institutions—public education, religion, government, the home, cultural foundations, and so on. But all of these seem to revolve around a central core of inauthenticity.

Naipaul's satirically barbed humor, then, has at least this one definite focal interest. His direction of approach varies, and his attitude, or tone, alters from book to book, but there is a discernible continuity in his presentation. This may be traced in the "ideal of progress" which, because of its false basis, causes difficulties for characters in every one of the novels. It is no coincidence that Ganesh, Harbans, Anand, Ralph Singh, both Henry and Frank in *A Flag on the Island,* and finally Bobby end up disillusioned and bitter. Though they move forward, they find no really satisfying rewards. Ralph Singh takes rather dubious consolation in having "fulfilled the fourfold division of life . . . student, householder and man of affairs, recluse" (300). But even though he claims to be preparing for more action, when we last see him he is in sterile isolation, hiding from life in a secluded hotel. The same malaise extends not only to the characters in *A Flag on the Island* but even to the island itself. In the name of modernity (progress) it has run up a bright new flag, catered to the tastes of the tourist bureaus, and ultimately lost its own identity. On the last page of *In a Free State,* Bobby's personal unfitness for aiding in the development of a new African state is put beyond doubt. Africa is not his home, as he has contended; he is an expatriate and is victim of the same colonial prejudices that have already driven many of his white colleagues out of the country.

Then there are the few—the narrator of *Miguel Street* to a slight extent, and especially Mr. Biswas and Mr. Stone—who have somehow managed in conjunction with their questionable material gains (or perhaps it would be more accurate to say in spite of them) to achieve a modicum of peace and satisfaction. The young man leaves Miguel Street, and he does so through bribery, but he displays compassion and a warm capacity for humor in his departure. Mr. Biswas gets his house; and though it is mortgaged far beyond his ability to pay he learns to control his anguish. Mr. Stone experiences a deep bitterness over the commercialized distortion of his projected ideal to rescue men from inactivity and preserve them from loneliness. But coming to himself after his lowest moment, he discovers respite in just having survived. He learns to bear his lot with stoic fortitude.

It appears from these and other examples that could be cited that whatever positive elements may inhere in Naipaul's works, they are definitely qualified. His satire grows more deeply serious, and the overall tone of his fiction darkens significantly with *A House for Mr Biswas,* but there is always balance in his expression. On this last point I must take issue with A. C. Derrick (who deplores the breakdown in human understanding and the "hollowness" and "lack of balance" of the novels), with Wilson Harris (who contends that Mr. Biswas' life never emerges into a question of spirit), and with George Lamming (who says that Naipaul seeks refuge from experience and cannot "move beyond a castrated satire").[14]

Admittedly, in the first two novels there is much low comedy; there are many farcical scenes, but there is too much consistency and development of plot, character, and other interests to warrant either the label "farce" or the charge of impotence for either work. Moreover, by the appearance of the more thoughtful *Miguel Street* it becomes quite evident that there is much more to Naipaul's humorous treatment than the surface reveals. "The farce has become a nightmare. Here [in *Miguel Street*] one finds it difficult to accept Lamming's description of Naipaul's satire as a refuge and escape from experience. If satire is a means of running away, it is equally a means of fighting; an act of bravery, not cowardice; the confrontation of a nightmare, not the seeking of a refuge."[15] With *A House for Mr Biswas* the satiric humor has become too prominent a part of the work to be taken lightly. It is even argued (with some justification) by Kenneth Ramchand, that Mr. Biswas' hostility toward the Tulsis is "in excess of, and prolonged beyond the rhetorical requirements of the novel" and that it reveals the author's own deep involvement with the people on whom the fictional creation is modeled.[16]

As for the question of spirit, the perseverance of such obscure little men as Mr. Biswas and Mr. Stone speaks eloquently for itself. No small part of the burden the common man must bear is his knowledge that there are seldom any "victories" for him in the normal sense of the word. Naipaul deals with insignificant men, but under his hand they assume importance. Their field of action is life, and he infuses their struggle with vision. In his article entitled "The Documentary Heresy," he contends that "true satire grows out of the largest vision" and that "out of the lesser vision comes the rape . . . which says only, 'This is life! Be afraid!' "[17]

In the novels it is true the characters show fear, and more often than not they fail to cope successfully with their problems, but this makes them all the more human. It is their "hollowness" and "lack of balance," not the work's or the author's, that shape the total impact of each novel. More admirable figures would be more attractive; less intensive indictments might be more palatable, but Naipaul understands people and their weaknesses, and he knows the uses of satire. His controlling attitude gains in effectiveness as he moves from the lighter early comic sketches to the fuller drawing of Mr. Biswas, on into the darkly reflective later works. Satirist that he is, he takes a close, hard look at his world and, employing his incisive wit, he proceeds to convert his perception into art.

The worth of his irony is that it enables him to examine his past without any sentimental self-indulgence. . . . Irony enables Naipaul to get down to the bare humanity beneath his history. Because he is dealing with his own personal past, his irony does not preclude sympathy but reinforces it. He is able to answer in terms of creative sensibility a question to which he could find no satisfactory academic answer.[18]

CHAPTER 5

Dominant Themes

I *The Faces of Alienation*

MANY significant themes emerge from the pages of Naipaul's fiction; several of them, and their variations, because of their emphasis or the frequency of their occurrence, appear to be more important than others. At one time or another the focus is on such subjects as rebellion, escape, identity crises, rootlessness, politics, the drive "to get ahead," and even sex. Adding to the complexity of some of the works is that each of these, in turn, lends itself to different levels of interpretation. On the surface, the stories themselves deal with specific problems. Second, they dramatize particular aspects of life deriving from the colonial and early postcolonial situation. Third, they have underlying implications which are applicable everywhere in Western civilization.

There is no disparity among these subjects or the levels of their meaning, however, because a high degree of thematic unity is maintained by the presence of one cohesive theme, one central idea linking nearly all the others together. Almost every topic Naipaul treats at any length, when reduced to its basic terms, ultimately resolves itself into the fundamental aspects of alienation. Though this necessarily entails a certain amount of repetition, there is no redundancy, due to the variety of forms in which the presentations are cast. A series of people in different localities and situations come to grips with separate difficulties and settle them according to their peculiar temperaments and abilities. Naipaul's method of development might be called "incremental repetition," in the sense that the overall impression of his extant works appears to build cumulatively, each new expression of a previous concept modifying and illuminating what has gone before.

This is not to suggest that individual novels do not stand on their own merits, for they do. What it indicates is the pervasive unity of the fiction; and over a period of time it underscores the consistency of Naipaul's progress as an author from the youthful comedies to his more seriously executed later works. Part of the reason for the interconnectedness of all his writing is the fact that he continually draws heavily upon his personal background. A *Spectator* review of *The Middle Passage* expands upon the special quality of the autobiographical element in his discursive prose. "Mr. Naipaul's journey is one of self-knowledge . . . he is too engaged and dispirited at the end to generalise his theme. But his book has an importance beyond the personal: it deals in microcosm with one of the modern world's major problems, so new and huge it has scarcely been formulated . . . more and more people lead secondhand lives, of no independent meaning or purpose."[1]

If anything, what is said here is even more applicable to the fiction, for in crucial respects the native colonial environment evokes only too readily the feelings of inauthenticity that Naipaul expresses time and again. After centuries of dependency on foreign authority, it is against great obstacles, both physical and psychological, that newly autonomous people must struggle to determine their own identity as individuals and as a nation. In the West Indies the usual difficulties are intensified by the widely divergent races and cultures that have been more or less arbitrarily gathered there. *The Middle Passage* gives insight into their condition. "Everyone was an individual, fighting for his place in the community. Yet there was no community. We were of various races, religions, sets and cliques; and we had somehow found ourselves on the same small island. . . . There was no profound anti-imperialist feeling; indeed, it was only our Britishness, our belonging to the British Empire, which gave us any identity" (43). This is probably the most immediate shaping force behind Naipaul's characteristic treatment of specific themes; yet it is not so much the source as the use he makes of his material that is of greatest importance.

The alienation I have singled out as underlying nearly all of his expressions shows up prominently, for example, in his satirical handling of island politics. Already in the last chapter

I have indicated much of the significance of this subject. The mystic masseur ultimately gives up his activism, cuts ties with the people who elected him, and sells himself to the bureaucracy. When Harbans is finally well away from the constituency which he has literally bought, he keeps his vow never to return to them again. After rising to the heights of local government, Ralph Singh is frankly relieved to retire from everything he has gained and hide away in exile. We are given to believe that the causes of these reactions are rooted both in the personalities of the men and in the social conditions which produced them. That the problem does not lie with corruption in high places is made abundantly clear; the sickness Naipaul depicts is not quite so superficial, and it is much more widespread. The Englishman Mr. Stone experiences it; then with islander Ralph Singh and Frank, the American in *A Flag on the Island,* and Bobby in Africa it assumes international dimensions.

II   *"Derelict Land"*

First indications of the difficulties may be detected in their natural surroundings which, when not hostile, are invariably inhospitable. The dereliction (a term introduced by Naipaul in *A House for Mr Biswas* and used again in *The Middle Passage*) of practically inaccessible rural villages like Fuente Grove and Elvira where hardly anything palatable will grow is matched in *Miguel Street* by the urban brick and concrete that have supplanted B. Wordsworth's tree-studded lot. Mr. Biswas survives a number of discouraging habitations, from the shack of his childhood through various Tulsi dwellings, only to die in debt trying to pay for a house that has already begun to deteriorate before he makes the initial payment. Ralph keeps feeling that he is a shipwreck victim washed up first on a desert island and then on the shore of some strange city; and in fleeing a hurricane Frank is compelled to endure the commercialized foreignness of the once familiar island of his war days. "Little leaflets and folders full of photographs and maps with arrows and X's told us of the beauties of the island, now fully charted" (155). In moving from the name and label-ridden Moore-McCormack ship to the charted and equally artificialized atmosphere on land, he feels that "the whole world is being washed away" (152) just as Mr. Stone does when all around him he becomes aware of mutability and death. "All that mattered was man's own frailty and corruptibility. The order of the universe, to which he sought to ally himself, was not his order" (158). In like manner, Bobby is forced to the realization that he has not found a safe home in his adopted Africa.

Disorder and human frailty are underscored by the incompatibility between men and their surroundings. The difficulties these characters experience with the physical environment are only multiplied in societal relationships. Bernard Kirkler correctly sees Naipaul's representation of the problem as reaching far beyond the typical colonial setting. "The real problems facing the emerging colonies—and not only the emerging colonies but perhaps other places too—are not only economic or political ones, but also those of creating a morally coherent environment, a truly sustaining culture, of making a world which can be deeply meaningful to those who live in it."[2] This is a point the novels continually drive home: insecure men without a viable basis of authentic values lead unhappy, "secondhand" lives.

In *The Middle Passage* Naipaul stresses the susceptibility of Trinidadians to imitation of foreign styles and tastes, their tolerance for any kind of standards, and their consequent lack of any reliable values of their own.

The Trinidadian is a cosmopolitan. He is adaptable; he is cynical; having no rigid social conventions of his own, he is amused by the conventions of others. He is a natural anarchist, who has never been able to take the eminent at their own valuation. . . . Everything that makes the Trinidadian an unreliable, exploitable citizen makes him a quick, civilized person whose values are always human ones, whose standards are only those of wit and style. (77)

This adaptability takes the shape in his fiction of comic eccentricity that denies personal commitment, selfish individuality that serves only its own ends, and unscrupulous materialism that justifies the means by the accomplishment of a set goal.

Pundit Ganesh's fate illustrates the foreseeable outcome of such an unstable society. Through the narrator we see that Ganesh starts out with rather vague but nonetheless sound

principles. At first he refuses to pretend to heal when he knows
he cannot. Then when he does resort to trickery—as he does in
freeing the boy from the black cloud—he is at least determined
to utilize his book knowledge and his understanding of people
to help them. Slowly, this begins to change. He thwarts Leela and
Ramlogan's taxi monopoly only to accept the profits for himself.
As money accumulates his scruples bother him less. This allows
him to gull unsuspecting tourists, to undercut the rival magazine
The Hindu, and to execute coolly the designs that result in his
election to office.

As the narrator tells it, a series of circumstances dictates the
crucial moves, but as Ganesh acts he is obviously no pawn.
As a child he protests against empty formality by exaggerating
his Brahmin initiation ceremony into ridicule. Later he shows
cunning and resourcefulness in his various dealings with Ramlogan. Then in his infiltration and destruction of Narayan's
political party, the results of his ingenuity are no longer subject
to doubt. He can and does exert himself; the problem is that as
his experiences prove himself and the world to be more and more
false, he adjusts his principles accordingly and is thus left in the
compromising positions that lead to his final disillusionment—the
humiliating governor's dinner party and the strike fiasco.

Since his values are not deeply rooted and he is apparently
so flexible, it might seem that Ganesh could extricate himself
smoothly from these last situations. This is not the case; he is
too acutely aware of the meaninglessness and the falsity of his
role. He is no better in the end than the defeated Narayan who
has also denied his own identity by assuming an anglicized name.
In certain respects, he is worse off than Harbans in *The Suffrage
of Elvira* because he has had to reject qualities that never enter
into Harbans' personality. The two, however, because they rise
to the top, are admired by such inveterate operators as Ramlogan and Baksh.

The Suffrage of Elvira and *Miguel Street* reveal even more of
the unstructured multiplicity that contributes to the rootless
atmosphere of the island. One of the first lessons Harbans learns
about Elvira is that he can rely on no one. For a while the
exploiter is at the mercy of those he plans to exploit; and they
take advantage of their power. Muslim, Hindu, Christian, elderly,

young, local entrepreneur, Negro, Spaniard—each faction, and a number of individuals besides, must be placated. Everyone accepts his opponent's right to deceive and trick to the best of his ability. Dhaniram only laughs at Chittaranjan's believing that Nelly will get to marry Harbans' son. Foam routs the Jehovah's Witnesses by invoking *obeah*, Baksh, of course, advantageously switches candidates until he has exhausted his game and then quite happily steps aside.

On Miguel Street, instability is the rule of life. Employment is severely limited and opportunities for advancement are answers to impossibly distant dreams. Popo, the carpenter who is frightened by uninformed strangers who question him about his work, is happiest when making "the thing without a name." Most of the men collect garbage, labor for the Americans, or loaf; the ideal for some of them is to live off their wives' earnings as domestics. The women and girls, often presented sympathetically if only sketchily, lead hard lives. Marriage brings little comfort and no real security since they can almost be assured of beatings and unfaithfulness. Promiscuity and prostitution seem to be accepted with little question. Laura, piquing the inquisitive young narrator's curiosity, manages to provide for eight illegitimate children without visible means of support. Her example leads him to generalize. "One of the miracles of life in Miguel Street was that no one starved. If you sit down at a table with pencil and paper and try to work it out, you will find it impossible. But I lived in Miguel Street, and can assure you that no one starved. Perhaps they did go hungry, but you never heard about it" (114-15).

With such a formless insubstantial society, it is no wonder that unconventional behavior and rootlessness develop. There is no recognizably secure ground upon which consistent institutions can become established. Those which are imported from outside are quickly mixed and perverted when adopted by people who only vaguely understand them. Thus, the confused religious conglomeration of Elvira:

Everybody, Hindus, Muslims and Christians, owned a Bible; the Hindus and Muslims looking on it, if anything, with greater awe. Hindus and Muslims celebrated Christmas and Easter. The Spaniards and some of the negroes celebrated the Hindu festival of lights.

Someone had told them that Lakshmi, the goddess of prosperity,·
was being honoured; they placed small earthen lamps on their money-
boxes and waited, as they said, for the money to breed. Everybody
celebrated the Muslim festival of Hosein. (74)

Distinctions between groups, and eventually, even between races
become obscured, and individuals are left pretty much on their
own to interpret meanings and standards.

III   "A Stage in the Journey"

It is stylistically appropriate that in these first three books
Naipaul depicts his easygoing, fragmented society by touching
only briefly on various themes—not that he forgoes development
—but in concentrating primarily on filling out character sketches,
he sometimes gives the impression that he is dealing with thematic elements rather than with full-blown ideas. If this is a
just assessment, it fits the scene he is presenting, but nonetheless it constitutes a weakness in his earliest writing. Though it
may be a fault, it is a minor one that is overcome in A House
for Mr Biswas. In this novel thematic elements are consolidated
and assume much greater significance. The rootless instability
that marks existence in the previous fiction becomes an intensive
dramatization of what it means to be transient.

The "derelict land" lends itself to exploration under a variety
of topics, but quite literally transience is exemplified at each
level of the action. It shows up in Mr. Biswas. "As a boy he had
moved from one house of strangers to another; and since his
marriage he felt he had lived nowhere but in the houses of the
Tulsis, at Hanuman House in Arwacas, in the decaying wooden
house at Shorthills, in the clumsy concrete house in Port of Spain.
And now at the end he found himself in his own house" (8).
It is important in the form of the disruptive changes that are
undermining the imported family arrangement of the Tulsis.
As a matter of fact, the family had never really intended to settle
in Trinidad in the first place. "Despite the solidity of their establishment the Tulsis had never considered themselves settled in
Arwacas or even Trinidad. It was no more than a stage in the
journey that had begun when Pundit Tulsi left India. Only the
death of Pundit Tulsi had prevented them from going back to

India; and ever since they had talked . . . of moving on, to India, Demerara, Surinam" (352). Then finally, this sense of impermanence is reflected in the attitude of the community as a whole, which is in a constant state of flux. Mr. Biswas' contacts with various layers of society in the line of his work bring out their restlessness, their aimless movement.

From the beginning Mr. Biswas displays signs of the same kind of malaise that ultimately drove Ganesh to his bitter rejection of the island. But his uneasiness is vented in a rather complex way and his more fully drawn personality gives greater dimension to his meaning. "Biswas is living to an extreme degree the anxieties of the uprooted man. His elaborate poses, daydreams, assertion of self and evasion of responsibility, are a result of the cultural social and psychological nowhereness produced by his position as an untalented second generation Hindu in poverty-stricken colonial Trinidad."[3] His struggle, like that of characters before him, is for a secure personal independence (symbolized by the house) that will permit him to live meaningfully. Ironically, however, since nothing in his environment has prepared him for this kind of freedom, he is unable to face the weighty responsibilities incumbent on self-determination.

In itself, this is a pertinent theme. As opposed to the stolid materialism of the Tulsis, Biswas' brand of egotism has positive qualities. Rather than ignore the hostile environment and lose himself in a tightly closed, unthinking communal structure, he attempts to carve a place for himself on his own terms. At times he has to relapse into the protective custody of the Tulsis—as after The Chase and after Green Vale—but romantic escapist that he is, he returns to a masochistic immersion in the very reality from which he wishes vainly to remove himself. His choice is of the lesser evil. The Tulsis' fantasy of solidarity is doomed to failure. They do not recognize the fact that their static little world is stagnating, with no creative urge, no adaptability, no will to test itself against reality.

That theirs is a false security is dramatically revealed in the dissolution of their establishment. They deny connections with the island, yet they have been too long away from India to have vital roots there. This is why, like the Bible-worshiping Hindus in Elvira, Owad wears a cross for good luck; their cultural identity is diminishing. Moreover, since no one is permitted to assert his individuality within the family, no one is allowed to "paddle his own canoe," there is no opportunity for self-awareness to develop. When Mrs. Tulsi's rigid control begins to slip, chaos ensues. Private enterprise in its worst form quickly devastates the Shorthills property. Simple repairs are neglected in favor of a series of abortive moneymaking schemes. Gardens, dairies, sheep lots are begun then allowed to deteriorate. Orchards are razed and along with most of the other good trees in the vicinity used for firewood. "W. C. Tuttle" fails at making furniture just as the widows' projects—selling liquor, sewing, peddling oranges —all fall through.

Apparently the Tulsis carry dereliction within themselves; whatever they touch is destroyed. Mrs. Tulsi's dream of passing the existing structure on to her sons is finally defeated when Owad like Shekhar before him marries an educated, modern girl from outside the faith and deserts the family in order to establish his own career. The mutual antipathy which exists from the first between Mr. Biswas and the Tulsis has nothing to do with their decline. He is just as selfish in a way as Mrs. Tulsi; he too wants to find stability in the midst of chaos, but he has the advantage at crucial moments of a driving compulsion to maintain what integrity he has and to escape into a more realistic environment. His rejection of the hollow and dying culture leaves him the *Sentinel*'s "deserving destitutes" and poverty-stricken Trinidad, not much of an alternative, but one that allows flexibility and the possibility of upward mobility.

In fact, it is his vital contact with the destitutes of Port of Spain that rescues him finally from the same debilitating lethargy that had kept the Tulsis isolated for years. "He sank into despair as into the void which, in his imagining, had always stood for the life he had yet to live. . . . But there was now no quickening panic, no knot of anguish. He discovered in himself only a great unwillingness, and that part of his mind which feared the consequences of such a withdrawal was increasingly stilled" (446). He is suddenly revived from this despair when, because of his unrivaled experience among the poor, he is offered a job in a new governmental department. "He had paid no more than a journalist's attention to all talk of postwar development, since he did not see how it involved him and his family. And now, on a Monday morning, he had walked into a new job, and this job made him part of the new era. And it was a job with the government!" (447). Briefly he has visions of security and prestige and advancement, but again his plans fail to materialize. This avenue of escape is closed when the department is eliminated, a victim of the changing times. "The department was abolished because it had grown archaic. Thirty, twenty or even ten years before, there would have been people to support it. But the war, the American bases, an awareness of America had given everyone the urge, and many the means, to self-improvement. The encouragement and guidance of the department were not needed" (527).

This late setback recalls him to his old fears and uncertainties, but it does not return him to where he was before. He has managed on his government salary to burden himself with his long desired house. In spite of his worries and the problems that never cease to arise, he continues to the end, striving to maintain his tenuous independence. Before he dies he even learns to appreciate simple things and thus avoids Ganesh's bitter fate. This seems to be a comparatively minor accomplishment, but it suggests the presence of something of lasting value. His unspectacular life is vindicated and given meaning by his will to overcome the dereliction and impermanence that mark his existence.

IV   *"To ... Anchor Himself"*

What the house means to Mr. Biswas the plan for the Knights Companion means to Mr. Stone—a stay against personal destruction. The Englishman's environment is not nearly so inchoate as Mr. Biswas', and his age and temperament call for a slightly different approach to the central themes I have been describing. With the change comes a shift in emphasis which brings out other aspects of alienation. Cultivating his long-established habits and calmly measuring the smooth flow of time by the passage of the seasons, he has lulled himself into forgetting about the unsettling aspects of life. A subliminal uneasiness has been growing within him as he approaches retirement, but his comfort is abruptly shaken when it dawns on him that loneliness, old age, and death lie ahead. Just the innocent wording on a transit poster focuses his attention on his latent doubts. "They recalled a moment—then, memory and fear quickening, he saw that they recalled several moments, which had multiplied during the last year—of unease, unsettlement . . . moments he had thought buried, for they formed no part of the pattern of his life" (25).

His quiet life as a bachelor has been perfectly satisfying until his security is questioned. Then all at once he begins to feel estranged from everything that had fit so neatly into his self-imposed pattern. It is too late, and the nature of his dilemma will not allow avenues of escape such as were open to the younger and more enthusiastic Mr. Biswas. His loneliness can be assuaged to a certain extent by marriage, so he takes in Mrs. Springer. Retirement can be made more pleasant, so he comes up with the idea of the Knights Companion. But the inevitability of death he must learn to accept. His coming to grips with transience is a painful process, but on his own terms he makes the adjustment.

For him rootlessness comes, not from the absence, but from the disruption of an existing order. Until he questions it, the environment seems to him to be a pleasant part of himself. The tree "he had grown to regard . . . as part of his own life, a marker of his past, for it moved through time with him. . . . All around him were such reminders of solidity, continuity and flow" (20). This changes, however, and he is at a loss as to what he should do. Margaret Springer offers an anchor of one kind, but the nature of his predicament is such that she cannot share all of his burden. To a great extent he is isolated, not only because of habits established over a lifetime of bachelorhood, but also because he has become acutely aware of the separateness of individuals.

He is more constantly sensitive to this feeling than Mr. Biswas is, but even in overcrowded Hanuman House there are lucid moments when the would-be rebel senses the loneliness of his position. "At Hanuman House, in the press of daughters, sons-in-law and children, he began to feel lost, unimportant and even frightened. No one particularly noticed him" (86-87). This is before marriage into the clan, but after Shama becomes his wife, he still finds it virtually impossible to communicate effectively with her or anyone else. There is a certain amount of immaturity in his loneliness; and it is significant that he often regrets the mother and the childhood home that he could never make a part of his life. At first Shama cannot be trusted. Anything he reveals to her might be used against him with the rest of the Tulsis. Over the years their relationship is loose enough that they even live separately for periods of time. Consequently, though they slowly grow closer together, there is always a gap between them.

Mr. Stone is naturally more reticent and more mature than Mr. Biswas, and in his unassertive way he approaches his problem by trying to overcome the differences of understanding that keep people lonely. His failure in the attempt serves all the more effectively to underscore the practical impossibility of his goal. Discord between himself and nature prompts him to bring Margaret into his life. Unfortunately for him, she can be rather unfeeling. After his especially depressing sight of a useless, retired man, she playfully chides him about the incident. Unknown to her, however, the scene has so impressed him that he has been motivated to take a second positive step toward alleviating loneliness and increasing understanding. Her dull response when he starts to introduce the scheme of the Knights Companion leads him to withhold his confidence.

> The words meant little to her. And she simply said, "That's very nice, Doggie."
> He fell silent. She did not notice it, so it did not develop into one of their silences. However, he resolved to tell her nothing more. (76)

For his own comfort he might have done well to keep his resolution; at another traumatic moment his wife again undercuts his faint optimism. After the death of Tony and the extermination of the neighborhood cat, and while he is suffering from the knowledge that his ideal of comforting the aged has degenerated into a public relations project, he conjectures aloud about the possibilities of human beings, like trees and grass, having a regenerating springtime. Margaret quips, "Well, I think it's a lotta rubbish" (147).

He also realizes after it is too late that he has been wrong in attempting to share his deepest feelings with his colleague from Public Relations, Bill Whymper.

Nothing that was pure ought to be exposed. And now he saw that in that project of the Knights Companion which had contributed so much to his restlessness, the only pure moments, the only true moments were those he had spent in the study, writing out of a feeling whose depth he realized only as he wrote. What he had written was a faint and artificial rendering of that emotion, and the scheme as the Unit had practised it was but a shadow of that shadow. (149)

The reference to Platonic idealism is unmistakable here in the contrast drawn between truth and shadow. Mr. Biswas could never find what he wanted in an actual house.[4] Mr. Stone cannot realize his dream; for in addition to his professed intention to help retirees, his latent goal is to create for himself in the Knights Companion a monument, something to perpetuate his memory, a stay against transience.

His quest has been a lonely one, but due to the fact that his personal problem is so basic to the human condition it raises his efforts to a symbolic level. Unable to communicate his feelings, in attempting to compensate for his inadequacies he simply intensifies his isolation. Nature, Margaret, Whymper, and even his own project have failed him.

There remained to him nothing to which he could anchor himself.
    In the routine of the office, as in the rhythm of the seasons, he could no longer participate. It all went without reference to himself. Soon it would go on without his presence. (149-50)

He despairs over the hostility of the universe toward man, and toward himself most specifically, but in the end he manages to come to terms with his fate. Stoically, he finds in the very fact of his survival reason to carry on with the process of life.

In *The Mimic Men* Naipaul returns to the subject of politics, but here again his focal interest conforms to the same pattern of development that has been emerging in the previous works. As the title suggests, the narrative is of men who, lacking an authentic, meaningful identity of their own, seek to give value and coherence to their lives by adopting the forms and manners of others. "To be born on an island like Isabella, an obscure New World transplantation, second-hand and barbarous, was to be born to disorder" (141). Ralph Singh and his compatriots view the foreign as the "true, pure world." "We, here on our island, handling books printed in this world, and using its goods, had been abandoned and forgotten. We pretended to be real, to be learning, to be preparing ourselves for life, we mimic men of the New World, one unknown corner of it, with all its reminders of the corruption that came so quickly to the new" (175).

Between the obscure, derelict Isabella of his youth and the sterile, evasive metropolis of his early retirement, Ralph is suspended without vital roots in either environment. His is the story of a vain attempt to secure for himself order and stability in the midst of confusion. At the heart of his difficulty is his personal detachment from the life around him. For him reality and fantasy are too closely paralleled, and he drifts from one to the other, unable to commit himself to either. In order to deny his makeshift island existence he turns to his imagination and his distant ancestors, the Aryan horsemen of the high, snowclad Himalayas. In his daydream he is their lost, shipwrecked leader, stranded in a foreign land.

Unable to relate fully to those around him, he conceives of himself as a performer in an absurd drama. His particular role is tempered by his renegade father who leads a minor rebellion in the hills of the island, reemphasizing for him the possibilities of greatness in his heritage. Thus, he acts before a hidden camera; his friends take their parts, and reality becomes a play which is subject to almost arbitrary interpretation. He states matter-of-factly that he and his schoolmates at Isabella Imperial are natural impersonators; and the roles they assume are imported from abroad.

I had been able at certain moments to think of Isabella as deserted and awaiting discovery. . . . The war was bringing us visitors, who saw more clearly than we did; we learned to see with them, and we were seeing only like visitors. . . . Our landscape was as manufactured as that of any great French or English park. But we walked in a garden of hell, among trees, some still without popular names, whose seeds had sometimes been brought to our island in the intestines of slaves. (175-76)

Distancing themselves from their surroundings only perpetuates the artificiality of their lives. Acquiescing to the stranger's point

of view is almost as limiting and degrading as the forced immi-
gration that brought many of their ancestors to the island
originally.

In the manner of Mr. Biswas, Ralph sets his mind on escape
from this corruption. He does not write romantic stories, but
rejecting the insipid present, he envisions a past greatness for
his people and a more significant future for himself. "I had made
my decision to abandon Isabella, to eschew my shipwreck on
the tropical desert island. . . . Now it felt corrupted and corrupting. It was this corruption which I now wished to flee. I wished to
make a fresh start in my own element; to rid myself of those
relationships which it solaced me to think of as temporary and
unimportant, but which I now felt to be tainting" (158). His
"own element"—identified in his mind with snow and a northern
temperate climate—as it turns out, does not hold the solution
to his problem. It is not that he needs to sever relationships,
no matter how temporary and unimportant, but he needs to
establish some which are genuine and stable enough to last.

For this to happen, his quest for authenticity must first take
an inward turn. Despite Naipaul's protestations against "searches
for identity,"[5] this theme is important for several of his protagonists, notably Ganesh, Mr. Biswas, and now Ralph Singh.
As a schoolboy, he is even more conscientious than Ganesh was
about the falsity of his name. "At school I was known as Ralph
Singh. The name Ralph I chose for the sake of the initial, which
was also that of my real name [Ranjit]. In this way I felt I miti-
gated the fantasy or deception . . . this was one of my heavy
secrets" (113). His father takes this as a sign of corruption,
and he is correct; it reveals rather than conceals the basic
inadequacy and insecurity that had prompted the name change
in the first place. Ralph cannot tolerate the commonness and
obscurity of his dislocated existence. Aligning himself by this
gesture with the more glamorous white world does nothing to
dispel his inner hollowness. The corruption from which he flees
is within, and when he tries to avoid it by immigrating to London
he merely changes the scene of his struggle. "Coming to London,
the great city, seeking order, seeking the flowering, the extension of myself that ought to have come in a city of such miracu-
lous light, I had tried to hasten a process which had seemed

elusive. I had tried to give myself a personality. It was something I had tried more than once before, and waited for the response in the eyes of others" (32). If anything, his confusion increases in the city; he no longer feels himself to be a whole person. This factor—more than the isolation and the loneliness—as it impresses itself on his mind, brings on panic.

V *"Extensions of Ourselves"*

For a while Ralph tries to locate himself and give concreteness to his actions by touring London, associating places and names, and by pursuing affairs with various seemingly anonymous women. From these unsatisfactory experiences he picks up trophies and gathers material for his "sexual diary." This frenetic movement fails to assuage his emptiness, however, and he then allows himself to become involved with Sandra, a girl who has no more sense of direction than he has. It seems that their mutual insecurity is about the strongest cohesive force in their mating. Soon after they are married, they begin drifting apart, on their way to the shipwreck of divorce.

Judging from the frequency with which misunderstandings and disappointments occur, it would appear that sex in general and marriage in particular offer very dubious comforts for Naipaul's characters. The treatment of male-female relationships in *The Mimic Men* makes explicit an aspect of his fiction that has been gaining in prominence since the earlier works. Ganesh quickly adjusts to Leela, but their marital relationship seems to solidify at a rather shallow level when it becomes apparent that she can never bear children. The narrator thinks it significant enough to mention that even when Ganesh administers her beatings it is without emotion, merely perfunctory ritual. Familial arrangements in *Miguel Street* are as a rule unstable and often lead to bitterness and fighting. It takes no time for Mr. Biswas to develop the conviction that he has been trapped by Shama, and as his family grows the feeling increases to an unbearable intensity. He learns, as does Mr. Stone after him, that he cannot confide in his wife. For both couples, there is little companionship and less understanding. Selma, in *A Flag on the Island*, fears marriage, "because marriage, for a girl of the people, was

full of perils and quick degradation" (189). Unwilling to limit
their individual freedom, she and Frank simply live together in
such a loosely structured arrangement that nothing but frustration results for both of them. This type of interpersonal malad-
justment ultimately culminates in the sterility of Bobby's homosexuality in *In a Free State*.

In *The Mimic Men*, Ralph's various sexual experiences only
serve to underscore the vast gulfs that separate individuals. A
significant factor in his total disillusionment is his failure to
achieve satisfaction even in the most intimate of human inter-
relationships. "We seek sex, and are left with two private bodies
on a stained bed. The larger erotic dream, the god, has eluded
us. It is so whenever, moving out of ourselves, we look for
extensions of ourselves" (22). A major source of his difficulty
is revealed in the wording of his complaint. He is seeking an
extension of himself in those with whom he comes into contact.
He expects an external solution to his internal problem. Unfortunately for his marriage he finds an extension of his own egotism
in Sandra's narcissism.

I kissed, caressed, stroked with hand and cheek; inadequate speech
was dragged out of me. "Lovely, lovely," I said. And Sandra had
replied, "Thank you." A cooling thing to hear, as I lay between
her breasts; and head and hands for an instant went still. But it
was a revealing reply, in its humourlessness and confidence. The
adoration of none could equal her own. (52)

This is taken from one of Naipaul's rare sensuous passages, and
the force of its impact is increased by the tempering coolness
that it lightly but firmly underscores. It is for good reason, long
after the marriage breaks up, that Ralph continues to remember
the cold kitchen and the empty rooms of their house in Isabella.

With Sandra in tow, Ralph abandons the greater disorder of
the city and pursues his search for identity back on the island.
At first they divert themselves with similarly disoriented friends
and with the accumulation of wealth. These activities proving
unsatisfactory, Ralph is drawn almost with relief out of his
lethargy and boredom into yet another false role—that of the
politician. In taking up his new part, realizing his utter lack
of power to fulfill its possibilities, he is caught up and swept

along with the drama until it leads directly into a confrontation with reality.

With their success in the election, Ralph, Sandra, Browne, and the other members of their group suddenly come to the realization that their playacting must be exposed. Ralph attempts to keep up the pretense by having everything labeled and named. "It suggested drama, activity. It reinforced reality" (257). In a short time, however, he succumbs to the falsity of his game; Sandra leaves, his friends break off in attempts to save themselves, and he falls into a noncommittal despair which allows everything he has acquired to drift away.

For four years drama had supported me; now, abruptly, drama failed. It was a private loss; thoughts of irresponsibility or duty dwindled, became absurd. I struggled to keep drama alive, for its replacement was despair: the vision of a boy walking on an endless desolate beach, between vegetation living, rotting, collapsed, and a mindless, living sea. No calm then: that came later, fleetingly. (263-64)

Again dereliction shakes his imposed order. It does not help him to escape again to London, to Lady Stella with her self-centered, standardized love-making, nor to seek consolation later with an island prostitute whose corseted and painted exterior belies the ugliness and fat hidden beneath.

Ralph eventually achieves a measure of calmness, but his final solution is fraught with artificiality. To find himself and give meaningful order to his life he turns to writing, parenthetically shutting off any episodes that do not fit the pattern he wishes to impose. With an ending that partakes more of Eastern philosophy than any other Naipaul has written, Ralph resigns himself to contemplative obscurity, thinking vaguely about the prospects for beginning some new "phase" in the process of life. In nothing that he has undertaken has he been able to realize anything like personal stability or fulfillment.

VI *"Move with the Times"*

Though *The Mimic Men* is another in a series of narratives which conclude on notes of frustration and failure, I would qualify A. C. Derrick's argument that personal failure is the dominant subject of the later novels.

The theme of personal failure dominates all of Naipaul's work after *The Suffrage of Elvira* (1958). The very process of defeat itself suggests the inevitable, that the outcome of effort could not have been otherwise than as demonstrated. Whether this inevitability is stated as in *The Mimic Men* (1967) or suggested, by the persistent recurrence of failure in *Miguel Street* (1959), and through imagery and symbol in *A House for Mr Biswas* (1961), and *Mr Stone and the Knights Companion* (1963), it is a recurring motif in the later novels.[6]

Failure is certainly a crucial motif; however, it is not crucial whether the several protagonists succeed or not. What is important is the fact of, and the causes behind, their inability to cope with either outcome. Mr. Biswas cannot be blamed for his poor health, nor can Mr. Stone for his old age, but success spoils Ganesh just as it overthrows Ralph.

As Ralph's political career illustrates, it is possible for certain ones to rise to the top; but once they have arrived and they begin to question their achievement the hollowness, the debilitating ambivalence within them, becomes evident, and they are incapable of sustaining the falsity. "Naipaul's characters live in a state of passive acceptance, from which they only rouse themselves occasionally; the temporary success they achieve when they are so prompted to action merely stresses the evanescence of the satisfaction and happiness that can be derived from attainment."[7] As this critic observes, it is the transitoriness of accomplishment that stands out in Naipaul's fiction. The characters that he portrays—alienated, without exception—are motivated primarily by negative forces and they lack purposeful direction. Ralph admits as much in explaining the reasons behind his political rise and fall. "Our grievances were our reality, what we knew, what had permitted us to grow, what had made us. We wondered at the ease of our success; we wondered why no one had called our bluff. We felt our success to be fraudulent" (240). The transience, the dereliction they seek to escape lies within: they are wise to seek order and meaning and their authentic identities, but as Naipaul shows repeatedly they stand little chance of finding lasting answers to their needs in material gains.

With only a minor shift in emphasis this concept is extended

and reformulated dramatically in *A Flag on the Island*. In the
name of progress or modernity the formerly obscure island has
simply given up one form of chaotic disorder for another.

> Once the island had seemed to me flagless. . . . The island was
> a floating suspended place to which you brought your own flag if
> you wanted to. . . . On the flagless island we, saluting the flag, were
> going back to America; Ma-Ho was going back to Canton as soon
> as the war was over; and the picture of Haile Selassie was there to
> remind Mr. Blackwhite, and to remind us, that he too had a place
> to go back to. "This place doesn't exist," he used to say, and he
> was wiser than any of us. (157)

In the interval since Frank's first stay on the island, nonentity
has given way; but it has only led to greater fraudulence and
corruption. From the alterations that have taken place, it is evident that what the islanders mean by "existence" is approving
acceptance from the outside world. They have purchased recognition and status by conforming outwardly to foreign concep-
tions of what they should be. Or in Blackwhite's words, "I think
I should move with the times" (219).

As I have noted in passing, this theme enters into several of
Naipaul's works, and it reflects a point he makes explicitly in
The Middle Passage. "Modernity in Trinidad, then, turns out
to be the extreme susceptibility of people who are unsure of
themselves and, having no taste or style of their own, are eager
for instruction" (47). In *A Flag on the Island*, foreign influence
perverts everything it touches: it makes Priest a regular television
personality, Henry the careworn proprietor of a respectable
nightclub, Blackwhite an exploiter of regional and racist literature, Selma a drudging suburban housewife; and what there is of
authentic island culture in general has been degraded into a
stylized mockery of itself. When Frank arrives at Henry's tourist-
packed "Coconut Grove" he finds the effects of these changes in
the floor show:

> Men and women in fancy costumes which were like the waiters'
> costumes came out on to the stage and began doing a fancy folk dance.
> They symbolically picked cotton, symbolically cut cane, symbolically
> carried water. They squatted and swayed on the floor and moaned

a dirge. From time to time a figure with a white mask over his face
ran among them, cracking a whip; and they lifted their hands in
pretty fear. (211)

Henry remarks on the scene laconically, "You see how us niggers
suffered." Again from *The Middle Passage*: "Culture is a dance—
not the dance that people do when more than three of them get
together—but the one put on in native costume on a stage. . . .
And nothing pleases Trinidadians so much as to see their culture
being applauded by white American tourists in night-clubs" (71).
   Everything has been commercialized, charted, labeled, and
packaged for consumption abroad. Frank, Henry, and even
Blackwhite to a certain extent realize their estrangement from
reality. They understand, but are incapable of reversing the
degradation to which each has contributed in his own way. And
awareness for them, as for Mr. Biswas, Mr. Stone, and Ralph
Singh, only adds to their bitterness and suffering. Like these
earlier protagonists, too, their reactions ultimately lead to rejection and a desire to escape. But for them, the dereliction
appears so overwhelmingly prevalent that only a gigantic catas-
trophe offers hope.
   It is fitting, not just for *A Flag on the Island*, but for the pervasive alienation that runs through all of Naipaul's work, that
this novel culminates in gestures of total denial. As the hurricane approaches, offering to sweep the island clean of corruption, the prospect is greeted with cries of joy. In the absurd
moment, the prospect of salvation through annihilation results
in courageous affirmation—affirmation that has been impossible
under the normal circumstances of life. Priest throws off the
commentator for the prophet; Henry recalls strength and manhood by defying his wife; Blackwhite regains his identity as a
person by accepting himself, not as black, not as white, but as
a human being; and Frank, "for me, no terror of sky and trees:
the courage of futility, the futility of courage, the empty, total
response" (233). Anticipating cataclysmic deliverance, they are
momentarily freed, but their moment is short-lived; afterward
they have to resume their burdens.
   Were it not for this sobering return to the mundane level of
existence here, the next novel, *In a Free State*, would appear

anticlimactic. But reality reasserts its force, and Bobby, having recovered from a past mental breakdown, attempts to establish a new, normal life in Africa. Undermining his efforts is the fact that he has, like Ralph Singh, simply transported his old self into a different environment. His instability manifests itself primarily on three fronts. One problem is perceptual; he sees Bergman landscapes and is unable to penetrate the inscrutability of the natives. Next, sexual difficulties show in the scene with the young Zulu and in his relationship with Linda. They compete as equals, bickering and changing moods like women rather than as man and woman. His aversion to her after discovering that she uses a vaginal deodorant becomes purely irrational. Then, in racial matters, too, he displays latent fear and insecurity. Repressed feelings of racial superiority come to the surface in his intimidation of the Africans at Esher and at the last when he finds his servant's laughter insupportable. Like Frank, in the end, he wishes to run away; but the solution to their fundamental problems is not to be found outside themselves.

Naipaul has developed this same concept in other books; and with each new formulation he broadens the applicability of his thought. Each outgrowth of the underlying alienation takes its own shape, but its relationship with the parent stock is there to be traced. Rejecting dereliction and rootlessness, one may seek meaningful order and stability through escape or rebellion. Yet, attempting either of these alternatives, even when totally unsuccessful, is likely to result in isolation and loneliness; if successful, it may still lead only to an inauthentic order, and the cycle of alienation and rejection is simply perpetuated. Naipaul, wisely, does not offer an outlet from the cycle, but he provides through dramatization a sensitive disclosure of the complexities which confront man in rapidly fluctuating modern civilization.

In his fiction Naipaul makes frequent use of the West Indian scene, but the effect of his presentation continues to overcome regional barriers. On the whole, he resorts to his island background in order to particularize themes that are really universal. To his advantage in employing this method is the fact that certain aspects of island life simply intensify elements common to existence in general. Louis James points out, for example,

that rootlessness is "by no means exclusively West Indian, but it
is intensified by the fact that uprooting here is often continu-
ous."[8] David Ormerod argues similarly in speaking of the imagery
of dereliction in Naipaul's work, tying it in with the middle
passage of former slave-colony days.

Mr Stone extends the image until it stands for the basic fact of
the entire human state—loneliness and helplessness, set against a
sterile landscape. Naipaul's world is one of homeless nomadic mi-
grants, making a middle passage from Africa or India to the West
Indies, thence to England and back again, for, after three hundred
years, there is no society and no system of values in which they
can take root.[9]

The implications Ormerod mentions are perhaps even more
explicit in the other novels that are actually set in the islands;
but another quality of Naipaul's style is also touched on here.
Concentrating on one seemingly inconsequential man, Naipaul
suggests truths that apply timelessly to all men. In effect, the
middle passage is man's passage.

CHAPTER 6

The Direct View

I *"The Regional Barrier"*

The social comedies I write can be fully appreciated only by someone
who knows the region I write about. Without that knowledge it is
easy for my books to be dismissed as farces and my characters as
eccentrics.   (Naipaul, 1958)[1]

All literatures are local. . . . The problems of Commonwealth writing
are really no more than the problems of writing; and the problems
of reading and comprehension are no more than the problems of
reading literature of any strange society.   (Naipaul, 1965)[2]

JUST over seven years stand between these seemingly contra-
dictory remarks, and in them may be observed evidence of
the direction of Naipaul's development as a writer. At the
time of his early complaint, *The Mystic Masseur, The Suffrage
of Elvira,* and *Miguel Street* had been written. Added to these
three books by the time of the second statement are *A House
for Mr Biswas, The Middle Passage, Mr Stone and the Knights
Companion,* and *An Area of Darkness.* His horizons have ex-
panded, and his increased experience has provided a confidence
allowing him to view what he had conceived to be a limited
problem as one of much broader scope.

Naipaul is right, of course, in insisting that knowledge of a
region will help the reader and the critic to understand and
appreciate more fully its peculiarities, but what he has come
to realize in the interval is that his problems may differ in
degree but not in kind from those faced by any author. The
artist must always face the task of overcoming the disparities
that exist between his and his reader's background and perception. This does not mean that differences are to be eliminated

147

but that they are to be made understandable within the context of what is being written.

If Naipaul may be taken at his word, his concern over the difficulties of communication between a writer and his audience began when he was quite young. According to his own account, he employed a method he calls "adaptation" to all the books he read in Trinidad. Thus, he adapted Dickens' and Eliot's London to a tropical climate and rejected their accompanying illustrations if they contradicted his fantasy. He was particularly assiduous in this endeavor because for him there appeared to be something almost sacred in the written word, and he did not like to have the absurdity of his myth exposed. "Fiction or any work of the imagination, whatever its quality, hallows its subject."[3] This feeling created a special dilemma for the ambitious young writer because his reverence for literature would not allow him to accept the possibilities of elevating his own surroundings by writing about them.

I might adapt Dickens to Trinidad; but it seemed impossible that the life I knew in Trinidad could ever be turned into a book. If landscapes do not start to be real until they have been interpreted by an artist, so, until they have been written about, societies appear to be without shape and *embarrassing*. It was embarrassing to be reminded by a Dickens illustration of the absurdity of my adaptations; it was equally embarrassing to attempt to write of what I saw.[4]

It was not until five years after he left Trinidad that he managed (at the age of twenty-three) to overcome his embarrassment and convince himself that what he had to say was important enough to be printed.

His local prejudice may account in part for the complaint he makes in "The Regional Barrier," yet in this article the immediate focus of attention is on a different aspect of his grievance. After having overcome his reservations and having published two books dealing exclusively with the West Indian scene, he has found it difficult, he says, to get a serious reading from critics and reviewers: "It isn't easy for the exotic writer to get his work accepted as being more than something exotic, something to be judged on its merits. The very originality of the material makes it suspect."[5] Of the misguided criticism he has met he singles out two examples. One critic says that his "whole purpose is to show how funny Trinidad Indians are," another that he "looks down his nose" at his origins—"We hope that in future he writes of his native land with warm affection." It is not that these comments are positive or negative that bothers him particularly but that, as he notes, "they are not literary judgements at all."[6] They are concerned more with the author's attitude toward his material than with the esthetic worth of his expression. As he sees it, their mistaken approach may be traced back to the fact that people are accustomed to reading about non-Europeans through European eyes and that the strangeness of the new writing misleads them. His emphasis later shifts, but in 1958, his rather defensive answer to critics is directed toward the authenticity that they overlook in his representation of Caribbean society. The implication is that knowledge of his accuracy should improve their ability to judge (whether or not it raises their estimation of his work).

His style, he argues, is not farcical, not exaggerated, nor does he resort to gimmicks to create funny "characters." The society he depicts (the one he describes elsewhere as picaresque) is without the conventions and restraints that normally make for conformity, and the surest way for an individual to make his presence felt is to be different. "Respectability and class still mean very little. Money means a good deal more.... For these reasons, Trinidadians are more recognizably 'characters' than people in England."[7] This, he contends, makes them easy material for the novelist; nourishing their eccentricities, they reveal themselves at once and obviate more extensive analysis. While this partially explains the apparent shallowness of some of his created figures, at the same time it serves to reinforce his opinion that the area in general tends to limit his artistic options. He writes for an English audience about an environment that is unfamiliar to them and as a result finds it difficult to win acceptance on the merits of his work.

Ultimately he concludes that he must cease to be regional and thus extend the appeal of his works. But of the available alternatives he rejects what he considers to be the three that appear to offer the quickest avenues to wide recognition. First, he cannot write about sex because the subject embarrasses him.

To center his fiction around a popular type of American hero
would be too patently artificial for his tastes. (This is nine years
before *A Flag on the Island.*) Third, dealing with racial dis-
crimination is objectionable because he suspects the underlying
motivation behind the drawing of ethnic conflicts. "I believe
they give a certain sadistic pleasure, a vicarious sense of power."[8]

Turning from these he considers the prospect of writing an
"English" novel, but he is discouraged because after eight years'
residence in London he does not feel that he knows enough
about England to capture its atmosphere effectively. Thus five
years prior to the publication of *Mr Stone and the Knights
Companion* he is confessing that London "is not a place I can
write about."[9] He had found the isolation of city life to be
depressing and barren after the openness and conviviality of
his childhood environment. "The profession I follow may be
partly responsible for this. Perhaps the fault is wholly mine. But
after eight years here I find I have, without effort, achieved
the Buddhist ideal of non-attachment. I am never disturbed by
national or international issues."[10] The detachment reflected here
is too similar to that of Ralph Singh in *The Mimic Men* to pass
unnoticed, and as it seems to appear in the novels, it becomes
a source of much of the strongest criticism that has been leveled
at Naipaul.

II *"The Documentary Heresy"*

Having decided to suppress his regionalistic emphasis, Naipaul
does not explain what direction he means to take; it is obvious,
however, from his next book, *A House for Mr Biswas*, that he
was not intending to exclude his West Indian setting and characters. In this his last exclusively West Indian novel, he indicates his change in approach through style more than anything
else. His purpose is artistic, and, as Kenneth Ramchand has
pointed out, he has adopted an approach that seems extraneous
to his countrymen—the satirizing of characters through the novel
of manners and morals.[11] While this has increased his critical
reputation abroad, it has not contributed to his popularity at
home. "Satirists are proverbially hot-water sailors, and V. S.
Naipaul—whose works have been a battleground for West Indian
literary and social criticism—is no exception."[12]

As a satirical humorist he has attempted to distance himself from his native environment in order to achieve the sort of detached perspective that is desirable if not essential to artistic expression. In this light, his attitude is understandable, but it has not endeared him to sensitive nationalists who are concerned about the image of their emerging countries. This is a sacrifice that Naipaul is apparently willing to make. His independent stand remains consistent (and rather courageous in the face of heated opposition, according to a report of his reception at a conference in Jamaica in January, 1971).[13]

In another context I have already referred to Naipaul's conception of the writer's "duty," but in this connection his ideas would bear further expansion. In *The Middle Passage* he argues that what the formless West Indian society needs is writers to give them shape, identity, authentic values, and a sense of direction, writers who are not afraid to employ the gifts of "subtlety and brutality" that are required. And he contends that thus far native authors have been too worried about "letting down their sides" to accomplish this positive end. "The insecure wish to be heroically portrayed. Irony and satire, which might help more, are not acceptable; and no writer wishes to let down his group." He goes further to say that because the West Indian author accepts the limited values of his special ethnic group he has "not only failed to diagnose the sickness of his society but aggravated it."[14]

In spite of these sentiments, Naipaul himself is not exempt from charges that he restricts his material too closely to his own Indian segment of the population and that he does not pay enough attention to the heterogeneous mixture of island races. In *An Area of Darkness* he takes up this very point in defending himself against, among others, George Lamming. He admits the accuracy of Lamming's conclusion that the confrontation of different communities is increasingly fundamental to the West Indian experience. "But to see the attenuation of the culture of my childhood as the result of a dramatic confrontation of opposed worlds would be to distort reality. To me the worlds were juxtaposed and mutually exclusive."[15] Arguing, then, on the solid premise that he must write out of his own experience, he submits that he has had to depend heavily on the kind of private world

that was rapidly dying out during his childhood. The record of
the changing order is vividly portrayed in *A House for Mr Biswas,*
and if anything the presentation is enhanced by the degree of
artistic detachment with which he is able to utilize his personal
experience in writing this book.

From his fiction and his more direct comments it would appear
that he is consciously directing his writing outward—still utilizing
what is closest to him, but formulating his expression so that it
takes on meaning for more and more people. As has been noted,
Mr. Biswas' predicament can be viewed as representative of
an entire culture in transition, and Mr. Stone is almost timeless
in his adjustments to conditions that face man anywhere. With
the expansion of his conceptual dimensions he also concentrates
less on defending his own position and turns his attention more
to matters of writing in general.

It is only logical, considering his ancestry, that Naipaul should
be interested in Indian literature. In *An Area of Darkness* his
overall disenchantment with India carries over rather oppres-
sively into his estimation of Indian writing. Their novels are
simply part of their "mimicry of the West," and he sees little
promise for the genre as they treat it. "What little I read of them
in translation did not encourage me to read more." Basically,
his objection seems to be primarily with their unimaginative
obsession with social issues. Premchand he finds to be a "minor
fabulist, much preoccupied with social issues," and other writers
bore him with incessant complaints about the sadness of poverty.
"The sweetness and sadness which can be found in Indian
writing and Indian films are a turning away from a too overwhelming reality; they reduce the horror to a warm, virtuous
emotion. Indian sentimentality is the opposite of concern."[16]
To one of Naipaul's critical temperament the right kind of "concern" seems to be extremely important. He returns to it again
and again in his discussion of other authors.

An Area of Darkness contains probably a longer list of writers
and his opinions of them than any other of his works.[17] E. M.
Forster and Rudyard Kipling quite naturally head the roster,
and both of them epitomize for him the influence of imperialism.
Kipling preserves the ambivalence of Britishers living in India—
people conscious of their power and separateness who are yet

fearful of the burden they had assumed.[18] In Forster's characters Naipaul detects an emphasis on their "Britishness," on a formulated ideal that has somehow reached a settled fulfillment—the kind of fulfillment, however, that he sees as artificial and stultifying. Its inherent limitations become evident in the consequent deterioration in the century's travel-writing. "We can observe a progressive deterioration, from Darwin (1832) to Trollope (1859) to Kingsley (1870) to Froude (1887). More and more these writers are reporting not on themselves but on their Englishness." Being overly conscious of their roles as Englishmen "limits vision and inquiry; it occasionally even rejects the truth."[19]

In this restrictive cultural narcissism Naipaul finds the reason that no contemporary English novelist, and for that matter none since Dickens, has possessed the magnitude of vision that could give form and substance to modern society's conception of itself. He contends for instance that the impression of London remains as Dickens left it.

On the modern mechanised city, its pressures and frustrations, English writers have remained silent. It is precisely this, on the other hand, which is one of the recurring themes of American writers. It is the theme, in the words of the novelist Peter de Vries, of city people who live and die without roots, suspended, "like the fabled mistletoe, between the twin oaks of home and office." It is an important theme and not specifically of America; but in England, where narcissism applies to country, class and self, it has been reduced to the image of the bank clerk, always precise, always punctual, who farcically erupts into misdemeanour. (207-8)

He touches this theme himself briefly in *The Mimic Men* (his next book after *An Area of Darkness*), but the point he makes after singling out this particular omission is that the vision of British novelists has so much diminished that not one of them has seriously attempted to chronicle as important a subject as the growth of national or imperial consciousness.

This would be especially important to Naipaul as a Commonwealth citizen since it serves in effect as a denial of the impact of colonialism on British self-awareness. His visit to India, as he shows in *An Area of Darkness*, only reinforces in him the

sense that people need to be induced to look critically at themselves to discover who they really are. This strong feeling could
have had an adverse effect on his imaginative writing had he
allowed it to distract him from his artistic purpose; fortunately
he does not let it get out of control. In fact, his reaction may
be seen to fit into a pattern which runs through his thinking in
the 1960's. During this period he shows a marked preoccupation
with what he considers to be a certain falseness and decadence
in contemporary literature.

Passing comments in a 1963 review article help to reveal
tenets of Naipaul's critical theory. He objects to J. P. Donleavy's
The Ginger Man primarily because the book has no social or
moral statement to make. This observation is not in lieu of other
artistic considerations; it is just that in spite of the novel's
occasional lyricism and other beauties of style, style alone is
simply insufficient to sustain the work. Though it is acutely
sensitive in some respects and elicits approval up to a certain
point, it fails to become emotionally satisfying. Part of the
failure, as he sees it, is that the leading character falls into a
spiritual vacuum, neither rising to the level of a hero nor
establishing himself as a believable "little man." "The high
spirits of the Ginger Man are fraudulent and unpleasant. At
their centre there is no calm, no hope, not even withdrawal.
There is only the void; and nothing will lead to nothing."[20]
Apparently, it is not that Donleavy tries to ignore the problems
of existence, but that he does not come to grips with them fully
and realistically. The point emerging here is not so much concerned with the justness of Naipaul's estimation, but with the
basis of his evaluative system. He has rather definite convictions
as to the responsibilities of the artist and the effect of his
expression.

Some of these ideas come out explicitly in "The Documentary
Heresy" (1964). This article deals specifically with Naipaul's
concept of the social role of the satirist; but to his thinking,
each artist is bound to impose his "vision" on the world. He who
fails to do so abandons half of his responsibility. From his
expansion of this conclusion it becomes obvious that he is not
advocating a facile didacticism; as a matter of fact, he is quite
successful himself in avoiding prescriptions for the edification

of man. What he is calling for is a change from the type of literature which fails to rise above a "documentary" reporting of reality. That is, in reaction to the heavy influence of naturalism he wishes to come back to a better-balanced, more unashamedly human expression. "The violence some of us are resisting is not the violence which is a counter of story-telling. It is the violence which is clinical and documentary in intention and makes no statement beyond that of bodily pain and degradation. It is like the obscene photograph. It deals anonymously with anonymous flesh, quickened only by pleasure or pain; and this anonymity is a denial of art."[21] The artist, then, is supposed to produce something meaningful out of brute reality and not settle for a mere presentation of the harshness of existence. "Out of the lesser vision comes the rape ... which only says, 'This is life! Be afraid!' "[22]

In the present age, he feels there is a degree of self-pity that is tantamount to "self-glamourization," as though men had not suffered and feared as much before the advent of the atomic bomb as after it. As he phrases it, the wrath of God may have been replaced in contemporary minds by a more mechanistic force, but the fear of death which is central to religious faith remains and "virtue continues to reside in great fear."[23] The only thing new in the present situation is the concerted effort to convert this elemental response into what Naipaul calls "an intellectual experience."

The result of this kind of egocentric intellection may be seen dramatically portrayed in *The Mimic Men*, but another article which appears in the same year as the novel (1967) contains more explicit discussion of the same topic. Here, Naipaul has taken the position that man's conception of himself has steadily diminished and that novelists have not only failed to retard the decline, but have actually contributed to it.

It is in the novel, especially, that we can see the steady degradation of man's idea of himself. The naturalistic novel of the 19th century, with its obsession for the details of proletarian labor, reduced man to a creature of simple materialism. Hemingway gave us the monkey-man of gross appetite, elementary reflexes and basic language expressing codified thought processes. Today's pretentious pornography and sadism go further. They reduce man to flesh capable only of pleasure or pain. They are a fair statement of the egalitarian age, since in the flesh unquickened by spirit all are truly equal.[24]

Further along he expresses contempt for the kind of equalitarian leveling which does not distinguish individuals from the mass, arguing that improvement must begin with the positive recognition of difference.

Citing his literary mentor Dickens, he asserts that what is needed is a heartfelt compassion and a direct vision that will make obvious the need for betterment. The right kind of "snobbery," a dissatisfaction with mediocrity, can be beneficial insofar as it leads one to desire improvement.

It comes from a recognition of difference and an abhorrence of it. Dickens was horrified by the low. . . . Orwell wondered whether this didn't mean that there was something "unreal" in Dickens's attack upon society. Unreal? We may ask whether Dickens's attitude— passion, snobbery and fear fully avowed, as it is in the statement, "I do not want to be like them"—isn't more constructive and in the end less corrupting than the doctrinaire romanticism which is used to fault him.[25]

To anyone familiar with Naipaul's work, this defense of Dickens will appear as only a thinly disguised apology for his own predominant attitude.

III   "What's Wrong with Being a Snob?"

From the evidence gathered out of his scattered criticism it appears that Naipaul's most common concern is with the "socially redeeming" aspects of literature. The pattern of his thinking is noticeably consistent in this respect. In spite of his rather strong feelings about the need for an "informing spirit" in art, however, he seems to be careful in avoiding specific pronouncements. He is certainly a reformer, but when it comes to his fiction he always utilizes the method of indirection that is indispensable to artistic expression. And in even his most tough-minded discursive statements, there is still room for reasonable flexibility. This is after all the only position available to a rational man. The field is, as he admits in *An Area of Darkness*, diverse and open-ended. "What does one look for in a novel? Story, 'characterization,' 'art,' realism, a moral, a good cry, beautiful writing? The point hasn't been settled" (226).

The mere fact of Naipaul's having expressed certain tenets, of course, does not guarantee their actual application in his own works. As it turns out, however, what he holds in theory does have a recognizable shaping influence on his fiction. Realizing the limitations of regionalism, after *Miguel Street* (1959) he deemphasizes local-color elements and brings out—as in *A House for Mr Biswas* (1961)—features of his characters and setting in such a way that they would have broader appeal. This is in keeping with his overt admission in *The Middle Passage* (1962) that the special situation of the West Indian writer deprives his work of universal appeal. "The reader is excluded; he is invited to witness; he cannot participate" (70). Then with *Mr Stone and the Knights Companion* he demonstrates his artistic independence of the island environment by transferring some of his favorite themes to suburban England.

In "The Regional Barrier" (1958), Naipaul states that London is a place about which he could not write. In 1971, he frankly admits the immaturity of this earlier view, but even before that his works reflect the increasing breadth of his intuitive perception.[26] By 1967 and publication of *The Mimic Men*, he seems to have gained enough confidence in his understanding of certain aspects of the metropolis to refute at least in part his youthful opinion. Ralph Singh's traumatic experiences with rootlessness, isolation, and inadequacy are quite pointedly shown to be peculiar not to any specific locality but to the human situation. A man can be cast adrift in the faceless city just as easily as he can in the forgotten provinces.

Another important application of his theory appears in his consistent emphasis on the need for spiritual rather than material growth. Through the nature of his characters' various mistakes and failures he vividly dramatizes this subject. Ganesh and Harbans are early gestures in this direction. Mr. Biswas' struggle with the Tulsis clarifies the issue; and the prominent stresses on survival in *Mr Stone and the Knights Companion* and *The Mimic Men* embody what might be taken as an answer to the deficiencies of such novels as *The Ginger Man*. Even in the depths of despair, and at times perhaps even because of their frenzied desperation,

Mr. Biswas, Mr. Stone, and Ralph are still capable of displaying
a latent calmness and at times, hope.

These three protagonists preserve for themselves the "jungle
clearing" that is so urgently sought by Frank in *A Flag on the
Island*—that position of withdrawal which is not negative, but
healing and soothing to the spirit. "And in my self imposed
isolation . . . I put on my spectacles and tried to savour my shrink-
ing, mortified flesh. But it was no use; the jungle pressed; confusion and threat were already being converted into that internal
excitement which is in itself fulfilment, and exhaustion" (151).
Bobby and Frank of the last two novelle are unsuccessful in attempting to bring their worlds under reasonable control, and
like their fictional predecessors, they seriously doubt the possibility of succeeding; but also like them, displaying the kind of
attitude that distinguishes them as more than simply flesh and
blood, they recognize the valuable necessity of seeking meaning and order. It may be that Naipaul oversimplifies in his
denunciation of what he calls Hemingway's "monkey-man" character, but the point he wishes to carry against the degrading,
materialistic obsession which pervades a certain type of literature is well taken.

There is little real optimism in Naipaul's works, and he constantly adheres to the factual harshness of reality, but he also
avoids overstressing the kind of fear "which only says 'This is
life! Be afraid!' " That would be false, and he shows no inclination to elevate his characters beyond the level of ordinary experience. Indeed, the beauty and power of his accomplishment lie
in his ability to capture and illuminate the deeper significance
in even the least of man's actions. Herein he ultimately hits upon
the most basic themes of the human spirit, transcending geographical and chronological barriers. Thus, ironically, in moving
progressively away from nationalism, regionalism and in the
strictest sense all but the most universal of "causes," he offers at
last what the widest-ranging among his readers might well consider a greater contribution to his homeland than is possible
from even the most devoted patriot. "In the end it is the writer
and the writing that matter. The attempt to perfect Indian
English or achieve Canadian-ness is the private endeavour of an
irrelevant nationalism . . . a country is ennobled by its writers

only if these writers are good."[27] The larger consideration, then—that of art, that which is durable and most apt to be valuable to mankind in general—takes precedence over shortsighted aims. This makes of Naipaul's works, in turn, one of the strongest cultural links between Western Europe and the Americas.

Notes and References

Chapter One

1. Philip M. Sherlock, *West Indies* (London: Thames and Hudson, Ltd., 1966), p. 7.

2. Kenneth Ramchand, *The West Indian Novel and Its Background* (New York: Barnes and Noble, 1970).

3. See W. I. Carr, "Reflections on the Novel in the British Caribbean," *Queens Quarterly*, 70, No. 4 (1963), 585-97.

4. Louis James, *The Islands in Between* (London: Oxford University Press, 1968), p. 10.

5. George Lamming, *The Pleasures of Exile* (London: Michael Joseph, 1960), p. 38.

6. These figures are taken from *The World Almanac and Book of Facts*, ed. Luman H. Long (New York: Newspaper Enterprise Association, Inc., 1971), p. 560.

7. Edward Lucie-Smith, *Listener*, 68 (August 16, 1962), 254.

8. V. S. Naipaul, *The Middle Passage* (London: Andre Deutsch, 1962), p. 156. Hereinafter quotations from Naipaul's book-length publications will be indicated, with page number(s) within parentheses, in the text. The bibliography contains full information on each edition from which passages are cited.

9. Ronald Bryden, "New Map of Hell," *Spectator*, 209 (August 3, 1962), 161.

10. "Mr. Naipaul's Passage to India," *Times Literary Supplement* (September 24, 1964), p. 881. On Naipaul's perceptive portrayal, see also Harry J. Benda, *Yale Review*, 55 (October, 1965), 121; V. S. Pritchett, "Back to India," *New Statesman*, 68 (September 11, 1964), 361-62.

11. On Naipaul's blind spots, see D. J. Enright, "Who Is India?," *Encounter*, 23 (December, 1964), 61-62; K. Gupta, *Canadian Forum*, 45 (June, 1965), 70; Raja Rao, "Out of Step with Shiva," *Book Week*, 2 (August 29, 1965), 14.

12. C. D. Narasimhaiah, "Somewhere Something Has Snapped," *Literary Criterion*, 6, No. 4 (n.d.), 90.

13. Henry Reed, "Passage to India," *Spectator*, 213 (October 2, 1964), 453.

14. Neil Millar, "Slavery's High Cost," *Christian Science Monitor* (May 28, 1970), p. 11.

15. Phoebe Adams, *Atlantic Monthly*, 225 (May, 1970), 130; Ronald Bryden, "Between the Epics," *New Statesman*, 78 (November 7, 1969), 662; J. H. Elliott, "Triste Trinidad," *New York Review of Books*, 14 (May 21, 1970), 27.

16. J. H. Plumb, "A Nightmare World of Fantasy and Murder," *Book World* (April 19, 1970), 1.

17. Richard Plant, "Potpourri of the Antilles," *Saturday Review*, 51 (June 8, 1968), 52.

Chapter Two

1. Karl Nyren, *Library Journal*, 84 (May 1, 1959), 1533.

2. A. C. Derrick, "Naipaul's Technique as a Novelist," *Journal of Commonwealth Literature*, 7 (July, 1969), 37.

3. *Ibid.*, p. 39.

4. David Ormerod, "Theme and Image in V. S. Naipaul's *A House for Mr Biswas*," *Texas Studies in Literature and Language*, 8 (Winter, 1967), 589.

5. Ramchand, *West Indian Novel*, p. 202.

6. For these two criticisms see first Sarah Blackburn, *Nation*, 205 (October 9, 1967), 348; then see John Wain, *New York Review of Books*, 9 (October 26, 1967), 34.

7. Derrick, "Naipaul's Technique," p. 43.

8. "Suburbia in the Sun," *Times Literary Supplement* (April 27, 1967), p. 349.

9. Karl Miller, "Naipaul's Emergent Country," *Listener*, 78 (September 28, 1967), 403.

10. Naipaul, "The Regional Barrier," *Times Literary Supplement*, supplement (August 15, 1958), p. xxxvii.

11. Miller, "Naipaul's . . . Country," p. 402.

12. "Huckster Hindu," *Time*, 73 (April 6, 1959), 99.

13. Naipaul, "Regional Barrier," p. xxxvii.

14. Wain, *New York Review of Books*, p. 34.

15. Blackburn, *Nation*, p. 348.

16. Miller, "Naipaul's . . . Country," p. 402.

Chapter Three

1. Gerald Moore, "East Indians and West. The Novels of V. S. Naipaul," *Black Orpheus*, 7 (June, 1960), 11.

2. In order to determine the accuracy of Naipaul's portrayal of

West Indian life, see Morton Klass, *East Indians in Trinidad* (New York: Columbia University Press, 1961). This book is the report on Mr. Klass's investigations in Trinidad from June, 1957 to June, 1958; it is not only informative, but a highly readable anthropological and sociological document, providing insights into many of the problems of familial and communal living that figure prominently in Naipaul's novels.

3. Naipaul, *The Suffrage of Elvira* (London: Andre Deutsch, 1958), p. 9.

4. Ormerod, "In a Derelict Land: The Novels of V. S. Naipaul," *Wisconsin Studies in Contemporary Literature*, 9 (Winter, 1968), 76.

5. Naipaul, *In a Free State* (New York: Alfred Knopf, 1971). Various allusions are made to films on pages 141, 162, 171, 174, and 223.

6. Ramchand, *West Indian Novel*, pp. 82 ff.

7. O[scar] R. Dathorne, *Caribbean Narrative: An Anthology of West Indian Writing* (London: Heinemann, 1966), p. 8.

8. Naipaul, "The Documentary Heresy," *Twentieth Century*, 173 (Winter, 1968), 108.

9. Hena Maes-Jelinek, "V. S. Naipaul: A Commonwealth Writer?," *Revue des Langues Vivantes*, 33 (1967), 501.

10. This habit could be written off as simply a Hindu custom—see Klass, *East Indians in Trinidad*, p. 102—but it certainly conforms with Beharry's generally submissive behavior pattern.

11. Maes-Jelinek, "V. S. Naipaul," p. 502.

12. See, for example, Wilson Harris, *Tradition and the West Indian Novel*, lecture delivered to the London West Indian Student's Association, London, May 15, 1964 (London: Telmow Press, 1965), p. 13; Derrick, "Naipaul's Technique," p. 38.

13. Gordon Rohlehr, "The Ironic Approach: The Novels of V. S. Naipaul," in *The Islands in Between*, ed. Louis James (London: Oxford University Press, 1968), pp. 137-38.

14. Albert Camus, *The Myth of Sisyphus*, trans. Justin O'Brien, Vintage Book (New York: Random House, 1955), p. 21.

15. Rohlehr, "Character and Rebellion in *A House for Mr Biswas*," *New World Quarterly*, 4, No. 4 (1968), 72.

16. Rohlehr, "Ironic Approach," p. 135.

17. Ormerod, "Theme and Image," p. 597.

18. Ramchand, *West Indian Novel*, p. 197.

19. Derrick, "Naipaul's Technique," p. 43. For further treatment of this subject see G. R. Coulthard, "The Literature of the West Indies," in *The Commonwealth Pen*, ed. Alan L. McLeod (Ithaca, N. Y.: Cornell University Press, 1961), p. 200; Dathorne, *Caribbean*

Narrative, p. 6; Mervyn Morris, "Some West Indian Problems of Audience," *English*, 16 (Spring, 1967), 128.

Chapter Four

1. Gilbert Highet, *The Anatomy of Satire* (Princeton, N. J.: Princeton University Press, 1962), p. 21.
2. Naipaul, "What's Wrong With Being a Snob?," *Saturday Evening Post*, 240 (June 3, 1967), 18.
3. See Lamming, *Pleasures of Exile*, p. 225; Derrick, "Naipaul's Technique," pp. 32-33, 38.
4. Ormerod, "In a Derelict Land," pp. 74, 75.
5. Naipaul, *The Mimic Men* (New York: Macmillan Company, 1967), p. 18.
6. Rohlehr, "Character and Rebellion," p. 72.
7. Rohlehr, "Ironic Approach," p. 126.
8. Derrick, "Naipaul's Technique," p. 35. .
9. Naipaul, *Middle Passage*, p. 41.
10. Ormerod, "In a Derelict Land," p. 82.
11. *Ibid.*, p. 87.
12. Ramchand, *West Indian Novel*, p. 201.
13. Naipaul, *A House for Mr Biswas* (London: Andre Deutsch, 1961), p. 397; *Mimic Men*, p. 110.
14. Derrick, "Naipaul's Technique," p. 32; Harris, *Tradition and the West Indian Novel*, p. 13; Lamming, *Pleasures of Exile*, p. 225.
15. Rohlehr, "Ironic Approach," pp. 125-26.
16. Ramchand, *West Indian Novel*, p. 202.
17. Naipaul, "Documentary Heresy," p. 108.
18. Rohlehr, "Ironic Approach," p. 139.

Chapter Five

1. Bryden, "New Map of Hell," p. 161.
2. Bernard Kirkler, "V. S. Naipaul's *A House for Mr Biswas*," *Listener*, 71 (February 13, 1964), 270-71.
3. Rohlehr, "Character and Rebellion," p. 68.
4. Ormerod in "Theme and Image," suggests the Platonic aspects of Mr. Biswas' quest for a house.
5. Naipaul, "Images," *New Statesman*, 70 (September 24, 1965), 452.
6. Derrick, "Naipaul's Technique," p. 32.
7. Maes-Jelinek, "V. S. Naipaul," p. 510.
8. Louis James, "Islands of Man: Reflections on the Emergence

of a West Indian Literature," *Southern Review,* 2, No. 2 (1966), 153.

  9. Ormerod, "In a Derelict Land," p. 76.

Chapter Six

  1. Naipaul, "Regional Barrier," p. xxxvii.

  2. Naipaul, "Images," p. 452.

  3. Naipaul, "Words on Their Own," *Times Literary Supplement* (June 4, 1964), p. 472.

  4. *Ibid.*

  5. Naipaul, "Regional Barrier," p. xxxvii.

  6. *Ibid.*

  7. *Ibid.*

  8. *Ibid.*

  9. *Ibid.*, p. xxxviii.

  10. *Ibid.*

  11. Ramchand, *West Indian Novel,* p. 5.

  12. Joseph and Johanna Jones, *Authors and Areas of the West Indies; People and Places in World English Literature, No. 2* (Austin, Texas: Steck-Vaughn, 1970), p. 48.

  13. One participant in a session went so far as to offer to shoot Naipaul. See Bernth Lindfors, "The West Indian Conference on Commonwealth Literature," *World Literature Written in English,* 19 (April, 1971), 10.

  14. Quotations in this paragraph are taken from Naipaul, *Middle Passage,* pp. 68-70.

  15. Naipaul, *An Area of Darkness* (New York: Macmillan Company, 1964), p. 37.

  16. Quotations in this paragraph are taken from Naipaul, *Area of Darkness,* pp. 226-27.

  17. Among the writers who receive at least passing reference are Forster, Dickens, Kipling, Thackeray, Hardy, Austen, Keats, Shelley, Hazlitt, Macaulay, Fielding, Maugham, Munro, Goldsmith, Stephen Leacock, Denise Robins, John O'Hara, Peter DeVries, Ada Leverson, Philip Woodruff, Malcolm Muggeridge, Tolstoy, Camus, Tagore, Nirad Chaudhuri, Premchand, R. K. Narayan, and many others.

  18. Naipaul, *Area of Darkness,* p. 201.

  19. Portions of this paragraph are quoted from *Area of Darkness,* pp. 206-7.

  20. Naipaul, "Castles of Fear," *Spectator,* 211 (July 5, 1963), 16.

  21. Naipaul, "Documentary Heresy," p. 107.

  22. *Ibid.*

  23. *Ibid.*

24. Naipaul, "What's Wrong with Being a Snob?," p. 18.

25. *Ibid.*

26. Ian Hamilton, "Without a Place," *Times Literary Supplement* (July 30, 1971), pp. 897-98.

27. Naipaul, "Images," p. 453.

Selected Bibliography

PRIMARY SOURCES

1. Books (arranged in order of publication)

The Mystic Masseur. New York: Vanguard Press, 1959. (First published 1957.)
The Suffrage of Elvira. London: Andre Deutsch, 1958.
Miguel Street. New York: Vanguard Press, Inc., 1959.
A House for Mr Biswas. London: Andre Deutsch, 1961.
The Middle Passage. London: Andre Deutsch, 1962.
Mr Stone and the Knights Companion. London: Andre·Deutsch, 1963.
An Area of Darkness. New York: The Macmillan Company, 1964.
The Mimic Men. New York: The Macmillan Company, 1967.
A Flag on the Island. New York: The Macmillan Company, 1967.
The Loss of El Dorado. New York: Alfred A. Knopf, 1970.
In a Free State. New York: Alfred A. Knopf, 1971.

2. Articles and Stories

"Australia Deserta." *Spectator,* 213 (October 16, 1964), 513.
"Baker's Story." *Kenyon Review,* 26 (Summer, 1964), 469-80.
"Caribbean Medley." *Vogue,* 134 (November 15, 1959), 90.
"Castles of Fear." *Spectator,* 211 (July 5, 1963), 16.
"Columbus and Crusoe." *Listener,* 78 (December 28, 1967), 845-46.
"The Documentary Heresy." *Twentieth Century,* 173 (Winter, 1964), 107-8.
"East Indian, West Indian." *Reporter,* 32 (June 17, 1965), 35-37.
"Enemy." *Vogue,* 137 (March 1, 1961), 69.
"Images." *New Statesman,* 70 (September 24, 1965), 452-53.
"Indian Autobiographies." *New Statesman,* 69 (January 29, 1965), 156-58.
"Jamshed into Jimmy." *New Statesman,* 65 (January 25, 1963), 129-30.
"Letter to Maria." *New Statesman,* 56 (July 5, 1958), 14.
"The Little More." *London Times* (July 13, 1961), p. 13.
"Living Like a Millionaire." *Vogue,* 138 (October 15, 1961), 92-93.
"New Novels." *New Statesman,* 59 (March 26, 1960), 461-62.

"Night Watchman's Occurrence Book." *Saturday Evening Post,* 236 (September 28, 1963), 72-75.
"Night Watchman's Occurrence Book." *Spectator,* 213 (November 27, 1964), 719, 721-22.
"One Out of Many." *Atlantic Monthly,* 227 (April, 1971), 71-82.
"The Regional Barrier." *Times Literary Supplement,* supplement (August 15, 1958), pp. xxxvii-xxxviii.
"Speaking of Writing." *London Times* (January 2, 1964), p. 11.
"Sporting Life." *Encounter,* 21 (September, 1963), 73-75.
"They Are Staring at Me." *Saturday Evening Post,* 238 (April 10, 1965), 82-84.
"Trinidad." *Mademoiselle,* 59 (May, 1964), 187-88.
"What's Wrong With Being a Snob?" *Saturday Evening Post,* 240 (June 3, 1967), 12, 18.
"Words on Their Own." *Times Literary Supplement* (June 4, 1964), p. 472.

SECONDARY SOURCES

1. Book Reviews

a. *An Area of Darkness* (1964)

BENDA, HARRY J. *Yale Review,* 55 (October, 1965), 121-23.
BISWAS, ROBIN. "Exhaustion and Persistence." *Tamarack Review,* 35 (Spring, 1965), 75-80.
BRAM, JOSEPH. *Library Journal,* 90 (April 15, 1965), 1904.
ENRIGHT, D. J. "Who Is India?" *Encounter,* 23 (December, 1964), 59-62, 64.
GUPTA, K. *Canadian Forum,* 45 (June, 1965), 70.
HITREC, JOSEPH. "A Disenchanted Journey." *Saturday Review,* 48 (May 1, 1965), 42.
MANDER, JOHN. "The Anglo Indian Theme." *Commentary,* 39 (June, 1965), 94-97.
"Mr. Naipaul's Passage to India." *Times Literary Supplement* (September 24, 1964), p. 881.
MUGGERIDGE, MALCOLM. *Esquire,* 64 (October, 1965), 28.
NARASIMHAIAH, C. D. "Somewhere Something Has Snapped." *Literary Criterion, Mysore,* 6, No. 4, pp. 83-96.
NATWAR-SINGH, K. "Unhappy Pilgrim." *New York Times Book Review* (July 11, 1965), p. 35.
OBERBECK, STEPHEN. "Angry Young Indian; Interview." *Newsweek,* 65 (April 19, 1965), 103-4.

PRESCOTT, ORVILLE. "The Land of His Ancestors." *New York Times* (April 16, 1965), p. 27.

PRITCHETT, V. S. "Back to India." *New Statesman*, 68 (September 11, 1964), 361-62.

RAO, RAJA. "Out of Step with Shiva." *Book Week*, 2 (August 29, 1965), 4, 14.

RAU, SANTHA RAMA. "Two Descriptions of the Elephant." *Reporter*, 33 (September 9, 1965), 40-43.

REED, HENRY. "Passage to India." *Spectator*, 213 (October 2, 1964), 452-53.

SHEEHAN, EDWARD R. F. "Cities of the Dreadful Night." *Nation*, 202 (March 14, 1966), 300-302.

Time, 85 (April 23, 1965), 109-10.

"Too Great a Burden." *Economist*, 213 (December 12, 1964), 1257.

"West Indian Writer Visits Homeland of His Ancestors." *London Times* (September 17, 1964), p. 17.

b. *A Flag on the Island* (1967)

BUCHAN, WILLIAM. *Spectator*, 219 (September 22, 1967), 328-29.

HARTMAN, JOHN W. *Best Sellers*, 28 (April 15, 1968), 29.

McINNIS, RAYMOND G. *Library Journal*, 93 (March 1, 1968), 1021.

MACNAMARA, DESMOND. *New Statesman*, 74 (September 15, 1967), 325.

MARSH, PAMELA. "Fiction Concentrate." *Christian Science Monitor*, 60 (March 29, 1968), 13.

MILLER, KARL. "Naipaul's Emergent Country." *Listener*, 78 (September 28, 1967), 402.

"Movietone." *Times Literary Supplement* (September 14, 1967), p. 813.

PLANT, RICHARD. "Potpourri of the Antilles." *Saturday Review*, 51 (June 8, 1968), 52.

PRITCHETT, V. S. "Crack-Up." *New York Review of Books*, 10 (April 11, 1968), 10, 12-14.

WAIN, JOHN. "Characters in the Sun." *New York Times Book Review* (April 7, 1968), p. 4.

c. *A House for Mr Biswas* (1961)

BAGAI, LEONA B. *Books Abroad*, 36 (Autumn, 1962), 453.

BALLIETT, WHITNEY. *New Yorker*, 38 (August 4, 1962), 70.

CHAPIN, LOUIS. *Christian Science Monitor*, 54 (July 19, 1962), 11.

CRUTTWELL, PATRICK. *Hudson Review*, 15 (Winter, 1962-63), 591-92.

EIMERL, SAREL. "A Trinidadian Dickens." *Reporter,* 27 (July 19, 1962), 56-57.

FULLER, JOHN. *Listener,* 66 (October 19, 1961), 621.

GILBERT, MORRIS. "Hapless Defiance." *New York Times Book Review* (June 24, 1962), p. 30.

JACOBSON, DAN. *New Statesman,* 62 (September 29, 1961), 440-41.

KEOWN, ERIC. *Punch,* 241 (October 25, 1961), 624.

Kirkus, 30 (March 1, 1962), 249.

LAMMING, GEORGE. *Time and Tide* (October 5, 1961), p. 1657.

MANN, CHARLES W., JR. *Library Journal,* 87 (May 15, 1962), 1917.

MITCHELL, JULIAN. "Everyman's Island." *Spectator,* 207 (October 6, 1961), 472.

"New Fiction." *London Times* (October 5, 1961), p. 16.

New York Herald Tribune Books, 38 (June 24, 1962), 6-7.

ROGERS, W. G. *Saturday Review,* 45 (June 9, 1962), 37.

Time, 79 (June 22, 1962), 96.

Times Literary Supplement (September 29, 1961), p. 641.

Times (London) *Weekly Review* (October 12, 1961), p. 10.

WYNDHAM, FRANCIS. *London Magazine,* 1 (October, 1961), 90-93.

d. *In a Free State* (1971)

CALDER, ANGUS. "Darkest Naipaulia." *New Statesman,* 82 (October 8, 1971), 482-83.

GORDIMER, NADINE. "White Expatriates and Black Mimics: *In a Free State.*" *New York Times Book Review* (October 17, 1971), pp. 5, 20.

KAZIN, ALFRED. "Displaced Person." *New York Review of Books,* 17 (December 30, 1971), 3-4.

LARSON, CHARLES R. *Saturday Review,* 54 (October 23, 1971), 91-92.

"Nowhere to Go." *Times Literary Supplement* (October 8, 1971), p. 1199.

e. *The Loss of El Dorado* (1970)

ADAMS, PHOEBE. *Atlantic Monthly,* 225 (May, 1970), 132.

BOROMÉ, J. A. *Library Journal,* 95 (April 1, 1970), 1367.

BRYDEN, RONALD. "Between the Epics." *New Statesman,* 78 (November 7, 1969), 661-62.

CHEUSE, ALAN. "The Realms of Gold." *Nation,* 211 (October 5, 1970), 311-12.

ELLIOTT, J. H. "Triste Trinidad." *New York Review of Books,* 14 (May 21, 1970), 25-27.

"The Failings of an Empire." *Times Literary Supplement* (December 25, 1969), p. 1471.

INNES, HAMMOND. "For God and Profit." *Spectator,* 223 (November 8, 1969), 647-48.

LASK, THOMAS. "Brave New World." *New York Times* (June 20, 1970), p. 27.

MAY, DERWENT. "A Black Tale." *London Times* (November 1, 1969), p. V.

MILLAR, NEIL. "Slavery's High Cost." *Christian Science Monitor* (May 28, 1970), p. 11.

MILLER, KARL. "Power, Glory and Imposture." *Listener,* 82 (November 13, 1969), 673-74.

PLUMB, J. H. "A Nightmare World of Fantasy and Murder." *Book World* (April 19, 1970), pp. 1, 3.

RABASSA, GREGORY. "The Dark, Obverse Side of the Shining Myth." *New York Times Book Review* (May 24, 1970), pp. 7, 22.

"Slave Colony." *Economist,* 233 (November 8, 1969), 64, iv.

"To Dream No More." *Time,* 95 (May 25, 1970), 105-6.

UPDIKE, JOHN. "Fool's Gold." *New Yorker,* 46 (August 8, 1970), 72-76.

f. *The Middle Passage* (1962)

ALLEN, WALTER. "Fear of Trinidad." *New Statesman,* 64 (August 3, 1962), 149-50.

BEDFORD, SYBILLE. "Stoic Traveler." *New York Review of Books,* 1 (November 14, 1963), 4-5.

BRYDEN, RONALD. "New Map of Hell." *Spectator,* 209 (August 3, 1962), 161.

DOLBIER, MAURICE. *New York Herald Tribune* (September 3, 1963), p. 19.

Encounter, 19 (September, 1962), 84.

GIOVANNI, NORMAN THOMAS DI. "Return of a West Indian." *Nation,* 197 (October 26, 1963), 262-63.

J., N. *Mexican Life,* 39 (October, 1963), 36-37.

JABAVU, NONI. "Return of an Insider." *New York Times Book Review* (September 22, 1963), p. 14.

JOHANSON, BERTRAM B. *Christian Science Monitor,* 55 (October 30, 1963), 9.

LUCIE-SMITH, EDWARD. *Listener,* 68 (August 16, 1962), 254-55.

MALAN, HARRISON B. *Library Journal,* 88 (October 15, 1963), 3842-43.

New Yorker, 39 (October 12, 1963), 213-14.

POORE, CHARLES. "A Native's Return to the Caribbean World." *New York Times* (September 7, 1963), p. 17.

Punch, 243 (August 8, 1962), 213.

"The Re-Engagement of Mr. Naipaul." *Times Literary Supplement* (August 10, 1962), p. 578.

g. *Miguel Street* (1959)

BALLIETT, WHITNEY. *New Yorker*, 36 (August 27, 1960), 98, 100.

Booklist, 56 (July 1, 1960), 654.

COLEMAN, JOHN. *Spectator*, 202 (April 24, 1959), 595.

MALONE, ROBERT M. *Library Journal*, 85 (May 15, 1960), 1938.

Manchester Guardian (April 4, 1959), p. 4.

PAYNE, ROBERT. "Caribbean Carnival." *Saturday Review*, 43 (July 2, 1960), 18.

POORE, CHARLES. *New York Times* (May 5, 1960), p. 33.

R., S. *Mexican Life*, 36 (June, 1960), 35.

RICHARDSON, MAURICE. *New Statesman*, 57 (May 2, 1959), 618.

RODMAN, SELDEN. "Catfish Row, Trinidad." *New York Times Book Review* (May 15, 1960), p. 43.

San Francisco Chronicle (May 22, 1960), p. 26.

Time, 75 (May 30, 1960), 79.

Times Literary Supplement (April 24, 1959), p. 237.

WICKENDEN, DAN. *New York Herald Tribune Book Review*, 36 (May 22, 1960), 10.

WOOD, PERCY. *Chicago Sunday Tribune Magazine of Books* (May 15, 1960), p. 6.

h. *The Mimic Men* (1967)

BELOFF, MAX. "Verandahs of Impotence." *Encounter*, 29 (October, 1967), 87.

BLACKBURN, SARA. *Nation*, 205 (October 9, 1967), 347-48.

CORKE, HILARY. *Listener*, 77 (May 25, 1967), 693.

CURLEY, ARTHUR. *Library Journal*, 92 (September 15, 1967), 3057.

GRAY, SIMON. *New Statesman*, 73 (May 5, 1967), 622-23.

LASK, THOMAS. "Shadow and Substance." *New York Times* (December 16, 1967), p. 39.

MALOFF, SAUL. *New York Times Book Review* (October 15, 1967), p. 55.

PLANT, RICHARD. "Caribbean Seesaw." *Saturday Review*, 50 (December 23, 1967), 32-33.

PRITCHETT, V. S. "Crack-Up." *New York Review of Books*, 10 (April 11, 1968), 10, 12-14.

PRYCE-JONES, DAVID. *London Magazine,* 7 (May, 1967), 82.
SEYMOUR-SMITH, MARTIN. "Exile's Story." *Spectator,* 218 (May 5, 1967), 528.
"Suburbia in the Sun." *Times Literary Supplement* (April 27, 1967), p. 349.
WAIN, JOHN. *New York Review of Books,* 9 (October 26, 1967), 33-35.

i. *Mr Stone and the Knights Companion* (1963)

ALLEN, WALTER. *New York Review of Books,* 2 (March 19, 1964), 21.
BROOKE, JOCELYN. *Listener,* 69 (May 30, 1963), 934.
CRUTTWELL, PATRICK. *Hudson Review,* 17 (Summer, 1964), 303, 311.
FRAKES, JAMES. "10K Golden Years." *Book Week,* 1 (March 22, 1964), 16.
GLEASON, J. *San Francisco Sunday Chronicle This World Magazine* (March 15, 1964), p. 41.
MANN, CHARLES W. *Library Journal,* 88 (December 15, 1963), 4789.
MITCHELL, ADRIAN. *Spectator,* 210 (June 21, 1963), 815.
"New Fiction." *London Times* (May 30, 1963), p. 16.
New Yorker, 40 (March 7, 1964), 181.
PRICE, R. G. G. *Punch,* 244 (June 12, 1963), 865.
PRITCHETT, V. S. "Climacteric." *New Statesman,* 65 (May 31, 1963), 831-32.
PRYCE-JONES, A. *New York Herald Tribune* (March 7, 1964), p. 13.
ROSS, ALAN. *London Magazine,* 111 (August, 1963), 87-88.
"A Short, Painful Life." *Time,* 83 (February 28, 1964), 110, 112.
"Sunk in Suburbia." *Times Literary Supplement* (May 31, 1963), p. 385.
WOOD, FREDRICK T. *English Studies,* 45 (June, 1964), 261.
WOOD, PERCY. "A Gem in an English Setting." *Chicago Sunday Tribune Magazine of Books* (February 9, 1964), p. 4.

j. *The Mystic Masseur* (1957)

AMIS, KINGSLEY. "Fresh Winds from the West." *Spectator,* 200 (May 2, 1958), 565-66.
BALLIETT, WHITNEY. *New Yorker,* 35 (May 30, 1959), 103.
BARO, GENE. "Ganesh's Beguiling Exploits." *New York Herald Tribune Book Review,* 35 (June 7, 1959), 6.
BAYLEY, JOHN. *Spectator,* 198 (May 24, 1957), 688.
"Huckster Hindu." *Time,* 73 (April 6, 1959), 99.
LEVIN, MARTIN. "How the Ball Bounces Down Trinidad Way." *New York Times Book Review* (April 12, 1959), p. 5.

"New Fiction." *London Times* (May 23, 1957), p. 15.

NYREN, KARL. *Library Journal*, 84 (May 1, 1959), 1533.

QUINTON, ANTHONY. *New Statesman*, 53 (May 18, 1957), 649.

Times Literary Supplement (May 31, 1957), p. 333.

WOOD, PERCY. *Chicago Sunday Tribune Magazine of Books* (July 12, 1959), p. 5.

k. *The Suffrage of Elvira* (1958)

"New Fiction." *London Times* (April 24, 1958), p. 13.

2. Criticism

BRAITHWAITE, EDWARD. "West Indian Prose Fiction in the Sixties: A Survey." *Critical Survey*, 3 (Winter, 1967), 169-74. Stresses importance of *A House for Mr Biswas* in the development of the West Indian novel.

CAMUS, ALBERT. *The Myth of Sisyphus*, trans. Justin O'Brien. Vintage Books. New York: Random House, 1955. Philosophical essays.

"The Caribbean Mixture." *Times Literary Supplement* (August 10, 1962), p. 578. Sees *Middle Passage* as first recognition of mutual responsibility between West Indian writers and their audience.

CARR, W. I. "Reflections on the Novel in the British Caribbean." *Queens Quarterly*, 70 (Winter, 1963), 585-97. Scans development of West Indian writing and important writers.

COLLYMORE, FRANK A. "Writing in the West Indies: A Survey." *Tamarack Review*, 14 (Winter, 1960), 111-24. Views significant writers and movements in West Indian literature.

COULTHARD, G. R. "The Literature of the West Indies." *The Commonwealth Pen*. Ed. Alan L. McLeod. Ithaca, N. Y.: Cornell University Press, 1961. Concise view of problems faced by West Indian writers. Summarizes dominant themes of area.

DATHORNE, O[SCAR] R., ed. *Caribbean Narrative: An Anthology of West Indian Writing*. London: Heinemann, 1966. Introduction recounts brief history of West Indian literature.

DERRICK, A. C. "Naipaul's Technique as a Novelist." *Journal of Commonwealth Literature*, 7 (July, 1969), 32-44. Traces theme of personal failure which dominates after the second novel. Unsatisfactory aspect of the novels in their "hollowness" and "lack of balance."

DRAYTON, ARTHUR. "West Indian Fiction and West Indian Society." *Kenyon Review*, 25 (Winter, 1963), 129-41. Centers on the middle-class, sociological aspects of Naipaul and other authors.

FIGUEROA, JOHN J. M. "Some Provisional Comments on West Indian Novels." *Commonwealth Literature*. Ed. John Press. London: Heinemann, 1965. Plight of West Indian of East Indian descent in *A House for Mr Biswas* treated accurately in fictional rather than documentary manner.

HAMILTON, IAN. "Without a Place." *Times Literary Supplement* (July 30, 1971), pp. 897-98. Interview containing Naipaul's reflective commentary on his works and career.

HARRIS, WILSON. *Tradition and the West Indian Novel*. Lecture delivered to the London West Indian Student's Association, London, May 15, 1964. London: Telmow Press, 1965. Concerned primarily with the area's tradition. Questions spiritual poverty of Mr. Biswas.

HIGHET, GILBERT. *The Anatomy of Satire*. Princeton, N. J.: Princeton University Press, 1962. Analytical study of satire in its various forms.

JAMES, LOUIS, ed. *The Islands in Between*. London: Oxford University Press, 1968. Collection of valuable studies on authors of the Caribbean.

————. "Islands of Man: Reflections on the Emergence of a West Indian Literature." *Southern Review*, 2, No. 2 (1966), 150-63. Scans rapid growth of West Indian fiction. Sees Mr. Biswas as archetypal fool.

JONES, JOSEPH AND JONES, JOHANNA. *Authors and Areas of the West Indies: People and Places in World English Literature, No. 2.* Austin, Texas: Steck-Vaughn Company, 1970. Profiles, bibliographies, photographs of representative West Indian writers.

KIRKLER, BERNARD. "V. S. Naipaul's *A House for Mr Biswas*." *Listener*, 71 (February 13, 1964), 270-71. Views Biswas' personal struggle as representative of entire colonial situation.

KLASS, MORTON. *East Indians in Trinidad*. New York: Columbia University Press, 1961. Sociological study of life styles in the Indian communities of Trinidad.

LAMMING, GEORGE. *The Pleasures of Exile*. London: Michael Joseph, 1960. Explores the plight of colonial writers. Accuses Naipaul of seeking refuge in satire.

LEE, R. H. "The Novels of V. S. Naipaul." *Theoria*, 27, pp. 31-46. Sees similarity with Dickens in "documentation of sociological phenomenon" and in increasing ability to control the vivid life being portrayed.

LINDFORS, BERNTH. "The West Indian Conference on Commonwealth Literature." *World Literature Written in English*, 19 (April,

1971), 9-13. Relates impressions of conference and audience reactions.

McLeod, Alan L. *The Commonwealth Pen.* Ithaca, N. Y.: Cornell University Press, 1961. Subtitled *An Introduction to the Literature of the British Commonwealth.*

Maes-Jelinek, Hena. "V. S. Naipaul: A Commonwealth Writer?" *Revue des Langues Vivantes,* 33 (1967), 499-513. Considers characters and tone of humor in novels. Refers to Naipaul's travel books and other discursive statements.

Miller, Karl. "Naipaul's Emergent Country." *Listener,* 78 (September 28, 1967), 402-3. Traces Naipaul's development from early series of social comedies to "jagged," "hallucinatory" style of *A Flag on the Island.*

————. "V. S. Naipaul and the New Order." *Kenyon Review,* 29 (November, 1967), 685-98. Stresses political aspects of *The Mimic Men* and the other works.

Moore, Gerald. "East Indians and West. The Novels of V. S. Naipaul." *Black Orpheus,* 7 (June, 1960), 11-15. Points up accuracy of observation and colorful presentation.

Morris, Mervyn. "Some West Indian Problems of Audience." *English,* 16 (Spring, 1967), 127-31. Enumerates practical advantages of self-exile for West Indian writers.

Nandakumar, Prema. "V. S. Naipaul." *The Glory and the Good.* New Delhi: Asia Publishing House, 1965. General survey of early works through *Mr Stone and the Knights Companion.*

Ormerod, David. "In a Derelict Land: The Novels of V. S. Naipaul." *Wisconsin Studies in Contemporary Literature,* 9 (Winter, 1968), 74-90. Explores themes of dereliction in the novels.

————. "Theme and Image in V. S. Naipaul's *A House for Mr Biswas.*" *Texas Studies in Literature and Language,* 8 (Winter, 1967), 589-602. Discusses structural consistency provided by themes and images.

"Pooter." *London Times* (November 8, 1968), p. 23. Naipaul a "serious comedian."

Ramchand, Kenneth. *The West Indian Novel and Its Background.* New York: Barnes and Noble Inc., 1970. Contains several passages of sensitive criticism of Naipaul's work.

Ramraj, Victor. "The All-Embracing Christlike Vision: Tone and Attitude in *The Mimic Men.*" *Commonwealth.* Papers delivered at the Conference of Commonwealth Literature, Aarhus University, April 26-30, 1971. Ed. Anna Rutherford. Aarhus: Akademisk Boghandel, 1971. Naipaul progresses beyond mere satire and

in later works analyzes characters and circumstances with increasing perception and sympathy.

RAMSARAN, J. A. "The Social Groundwork of Politics in Some West
Indian Novels." *Negro Digest*, 18 (August, 1969), 71-77. Deals
with political motivations in certain novels.

ROHLEHR, GORDON. "Character and Rebellion in *A House for Mr
Biswas*." *New World Quarterly*, 4, No. 4 (1968), 66-72. Archetypal nature of Mr. Biswas' struggle against rootlessness.

—————. "The Ironic Approach: The Novels of V. S. Naipaul." *The
Islands in Between*. Ed. Louis James. London: Oxford Press,
1968. Sees irony as source of Naipaul's artistic power.

SHENKER, ISRAEL. "V. S. Naipaul, Man Without a Society." *New
York Times Book Review* (October 17, 1971), pp. 4, 22-24.
Biographical. Quotes Naipaul as to his growth in international
awareness and his readiness now to give up writing.

SHERLOCK, PHILIP M. *West Indies*. London: Thames and Hudson
Ltd., 1966. Notes general themes of West Indian literature and
comments on Naipaul's eye for the ludicrous.

THORPE, MARJORIE. "*The Mimic Men*: A Study in Isolation." *New
World Quarterly*, 4, No. 4 (1968), 55-59. Reasserts Naipaul's
basic pessimism.

WYNTER, SYLVIA. "Reflections on West Indian Writing and Criticism."
Jamaica Journal, 2, No. 4, pp. 22-32. As part of larger scheme,
relates Naipaul to other West Indian writers and critics.

Index

179

DATE DUE

MAR. 17			
GAYLORD			PRINTED IN U.S.A.